(∧

MW00979339

"I didn't read this because I've been dead for years!"
Albert Einstein, Scientist

"Stop...asking me...for book blurb.....please get the antidote! It's just on the counter....please...I beg of you. No time left..."
James Magnus, Chemist

"I really enjoyed reading this book and appreciate that it functions both as a print object and as a digital curio! Great price points, too."
Reggie, A Sentient Blog Of Slime That Recently Took Control Of The Lab

---

"I wish I'd read this book. It would have been so much easier than learning about DNA!"
James Watson and Francis Crick, at the same time

Watch for future titles in the
Make Your Own Mistakes series.
There are countless mistakes to make!

Ask your bookseller for books you have missed, or
ask your friends and family to buy them for you as
presents. If that doesn't work, ask them for a gift
card and then use the gift card to buy more books.

Learn more about the lab at FakeScience.org.

YOU'RE A SCIENTIST by PHIL EDWARDS

YOU'RE A SCIENTIST!

BY PHIL EDWARDS
Chief Transcriptionist for the
FAKE SCIENCE LABS

ILLUSTRATED BY A TEAM OF HUNDREDS

This volume is dedicated to all the victims of our science.

YOU HAVE BEEN WARNED

This book is like no other you've ever read, unless this is your second time reading this book.

You will MAKE the MISTAKES that happen in the story. No one will decide for you.

Countless things can go wrong, and you determine which ones occur. Your decision making and page turning abilities will be tested. The consequence of a wrong decision? Your story will end, unless you turn back and start anew.

You're about to become a scientist. Will you make it big? Or will you make it medium or small? Only you can MAKE YOUR OWN MISTAKES in the world of science.

Good luck in your journey!

You did it!

After an incredibly thorough hiring process, you're finally here: The Fake Science Laboratories! Yep, they're the same ones you might recognize from that asbestos roller skate lawsuit last year.

You've read the lab's history a hundred times: *Founded in 1822 by Doctor Addison Kellogg Faken, he never told his employees he wasn't actually a doctor, but he did drop the "n" from his name to protect his family's reputation. Thus the Fake Science Lab was born, though only figuratively, since Dr. Faken never did learn how babies were made.*

Now it's a giant conglomerate with hundreds of laboratories in suburbs around the world. And you're going to be part of it!

You take in a deep breath, partly from exhilaration and partly because the air quality around the lab is so poor (all the squirrels you've seen are gasping).

It feels great to get to work, but who knew it would be so hard to find a job as a beaker cleaner, especially after you earned a graduate degree in flask cleaning? Still, now you have it, and it's time to get to work.

You pass through a set of wide, fingerprint-smudged glass doors and walk over a cool tile floor. The receptionist smiles and directs you to Lab A348, and you can't help but think it's fate: A348 is your lucky number!

Turn to the next page.

Once inside, you know what to do—you've trained for years to have this opportunity. It's time to follow your passion and clean some beakers.

You pull out your favorite beaker sponge, Beatram, and dunk your hand in a vat of hydrogen peroxide. Productivity stings so good!

You're in the zone now, so you call HQ with a request for your favorite cleaning agent: baking soda. There's something so wonderful about the old-fashioned methods.

Just as you're about to give Beatram the ride of his life, a strange woman appears at the door. She speaks with a vaguely European accent.

"You! Come with me. You just got a promotion!"

B looking good!

Beatram during your trip to Paris last summer. He looked so at home in front of the Eiffel Tower!

You gasp with excitement.

"Your accent is so stereotypical for an intelligent-yet-slightly-threatening authority figure. What country are you from?"

"There is no time," she says. "We must hurry. You're a scientist!"

"What about my beakers? What about my sponge?"

You stare at Beatram, but the scientist beckons to you. You realize that you've arrived at a crossroads: you're about to turn a page in your life, or at least a page in a book about your life. It's time to decide what to do.

Will you clean beakers and turn away from a life of discovery, where you could advance human knowledge forever, or at least amass a patent portfolio that could provide litigators with steady work?

Or will you become a scientist, with far greater responsibilities than cuddling with Beatram after a long day of work, feeling his moist and porous body caress your aching shins?

To ignore the woman and spend some quality time cleaning beakers with Beatram, turn to page 4.

To follow the woman with the stereotypical, but intelligent-sounding, accent, turn to page 5.

"Never mind," you say, your voice shaking. "I don't need baking soda. I'll make do with the hydrogen peroxide. I'm going to follow my passion."

"Beaker cleaning?" she says with a lilt.

"Beaker cleaning. With Beatram."

"Fine!" she shouts. "I shall find someone else, and you'll never find out what country my accent is from!"

You take Beatram in your hands and gaze upon the shelves of dirty beakers. So many beakers to clean, so little time!

You dunk him in the hydrogen peroxide and begin, and as you dunk and clean, the minutes fade to hours, and the hours fade to days. You feel yourself growing older, but you don't care as long as Beatram is at your side. Empires rise and fall, mankind ascends and descends history's long arc, but you are always there, with your favorite sponge, cleaning beakers until they are soiled again and wait for your touch alone.

You die with Beatram in your hands eighty years later. The lab mortician remarks that both of you are the most sterile-smelling things he's ever buried. He doesn't even need to use formaldehyde.

THE END

"I'm in," you say hesitantly. "But I'm taking Beatram with me."

"What are you talking about?" the scientist asks, her accent sounding even vaguer than before.

"Don't worry about it," you say as you plunge Beatram inside your pocket.

You follow the scientist through metal doors and into a large hallway overlooking the entire lab. Thousands of scientists scurry below you, their bodies so small that they hardly seem human.

"They look like ants from here," you tell the scientist.

"Are you joking? You know this is the myrmecology lab, don't you?"

This scientist uses such big words. You and Beatram will have a good laugh about her later over a glass of soda pop and baking soda pop.

"Follow me," she says, leading you past the tiny scientists who continue to scurry along the floor.

"Where are we going?"

She turns and raises an eyebrow.

"You have to decide your trade."

You swallow and follow her, and you run so fast that at one point you accidentally step on a tiny scientist. You tell the vaguely European scientist, worried about what might happen.

"You passed the intelligence test?" she asks.

"I like beakers and Beatram!" you shout. She continues down the hallway and turns a corner. You

Turn to the next page.

don't believe what you see on the other side.

The hall diverges into five distinct paths, all conveniently labeled for you. Everything looks so difficult.

"I'm scared," you say. "I'm going to clean beakers again."

"No you aren't!" the scientist says, plunging her hand into your pocket and pulling Beatram out. "I'll take this. You won't need it."

Beatram says nothing, but you can sense that he's in pain.

"Give him back now!" you cry.

"I will. But first, you must become a scientist."

"Fine, what do you want me to do?"

"I want you to choose."

She points at the doorways—now you must go through one if you ever hope to see Beatram again.

To explore space, turn to page 7.

To become a biologist, turn to page 9.

To become a chemist, turn to page 10.

To become an earth scientist, turn to page 11.

To become a physicist, turn to page 13.

Space! You run through the door and enter a beautiful planetarium. The stars look like ants from here, speckled across the canvas of our universe. A bespectacled man taps you on the shoulder.

"Ignore those. They escaped from the myrmecology lab."

You turn to your new boss—his name tag says Dr. Masterson, and you already know who he is. Just last year, he announced that Pluto was not actually a planet, but a small solid mass made of chocolate. It set the media and astronomy communities afire, especially when they considered the possibilities of Pluto fondue. Though it ultimately turned out to be a smudge on his telescope (from, fittingly enough, a Mars bar), Dr. Masterson had successfully established his reputation as a leader in the field.

"Why are you here?" he asks you, flicking a small piece of chocolate off his lab coat.

"I'm a beaker cleaner, sir, but the vaguely European woman said there was a major shortage of scientists."

"Yes, that's true, most of them were scared off by the rumors."

"Why would someone spread lies about the lab?"

"Actually, most of them are true." He beckons to you. "Follow me. I have a couple of jobs for you."

You follow Dr. Masterson through to the real planetarium and marvel at the constellations above.

"Right there, that's Orion's belt, isn't it?"

Turn to the next page.

"Actually, that's a ceiling tile. You know, the planetarium only works when we turn it on. Let's get to business. Do you want to be an astronaut? Or would you rather be an astronomer?"

You gulp and swallow—it's difficult to remember which is which. These are the types of questions Beatram always knew how to answer.

"It's so hard to choose," you say. "Remind me about the differences, why don't you?"

He pulls a chocolate bar from his pocket and unwraps it with a surprisingly delicate touch.

"My friend, it is simple. An astronomer looks at space while an astronaut dies in it. Once you choose, I'll give you your assignment."

"And then you'll give me back Beatram?"

"I have literally no idea what you're talking about. But the choice is yours. Are you brave enough to make it?"

He's waiting on you to decide.

To become an astronaut, turn to page 16.

To become an astronomer, turn to page 18.

Biology! You've heard so much about this -ology already, so why not try it for a spin?

Life itself, the thing you spend so much time trying to avoid, is going to become your playground. You run down the hallway and immediately slip. When you come to, tiny scientists are crawling all over you. A stern woman (not vaguely European) shouts down.

"Get those ants off you now. The myrmecology lab needs them."

You brush the tiny scientists off your body and follow her down the hallway. She walks with steely confidence, and you imitate her perfectly except for all the times you trip. Finally you reach it: the laboratory. The woman explains it all.

"Here we are. Since all my staff has left due to the lawsuits, radioactive cafeteria food, and substandard 401(k) policies, you're going to be one of our top biologists."

"So wait a second," you say, "just how many (k)s do you have? I need at least 100(k)s."

She sighs and brushes a tiny scientist off her shoulder.

"As enlightening as this discussion is, I really can't be bothered with it. I have to sedate some guinea pigs. So tell me: will you study animal or plant life?"

You feel a cold sweat, because it's time to decide, and because you dropped your hand in a jar labeled *Frozen Sweat Samples*.

To become a plant biologist, turn to page 20.

To become an animal biologist, turn to page 22.

10

Chemistry is your top choice—and to think that they told you *not* to drink from those bottles under the kitchen sink!

You proceed down the hallway, but your entrance to the world of chemistry is bittersweet. Already, you're surrounded by beakers, so you've never missed Beatram more. While you're staring at one beaker, a short man with large glasses appears, his face refracted in the glass.

"So!" he says. "You are my new chemist. What are your qualifications?"

"Well, I walked down a hallway."

"Wonderful!" He emerges from behind the beaker. "Are you interested in organic or inorganic chemistry?"

"Which one has more beakers?"

"That depends," he says. "Are you good at math?"

"Like counting?"

"Let's have you do some experiments." He rests a clammy hand on your shoulder. "Since my entire staff fled the building, there's a lot for you to do. What are you interested in?"

"Chemicals!" you shout, and he hands you two folders.

"Then choose, my chemically friend."

To take the folder labeled Baking Soda,
turn to page 23.

To take the folder labeled Explosive Poison?,
turn to page 24.

You're going to be an earth scientist! As soon as you run down the hallway, you know you've made the right choice—there are so many rocks to look at.

Big rocks, little rocks, medium rocks: the rocks are endless, and they're all assembled in a pile in the center of a large, dirty room. You're digging through them when a kind-faced scientist approaches you, his hair held back by a bandana that might actually be a repurposed napkin from the lab cafeteria.

"Nice pick," he says and points at the rock you're holding. "Igneous."

"Hey," you shoot back, "I know I'm not the smartest bulb in the tool shed, but there's no reason to call me igneous!"

"Igneous, not ignorant."

"Did you just do it again?"

He sighs.

"What's your name?"

You tell him your name and describe the busy day you've been having. He pulls back his bandana and you can clearly see that it's a napkin from a nearby fast food restaurant.

"So you're my new earth scientist. You think ants are tiny scientists, and you're obsessed with a beaker sponge."

"He has a name, you clod."

"I'll get you that sponge back. But I need some help. You see, I have some very important dirt-related science that only you can help me with."

Turn to the next page.

You follow him into a room with even more dirt in it. So much of life is disappointing, but earth science is really living up to your expectations. Still, it makes you a little sad to think how much fun Beatram would have had cleaning all this dirt. The scientist gestures toward the pile, his napkin bandana almost transparent from sweat.

"Count the dirt."

"How do you count dirt?"

"I want you to take each grain of dirt—we call them CDUs in the business. Certified Dirt Units."

It's a massive pile of dirt and you can't imagine how many CDUs you'll have to log. Plus, you never did go to that counting seminar you signed up for in graduate school (they made the mistake of putting it in a very high-numbered room).

Just as you're about to begin, you hear a burbling noise from behind a door labeled *Top Secret: Ignore That Burbling Noise*. It looks like your decision just got a little more difficult.

To continue counting dirt, turn to page 25.

To go through the mysterious and exciting door, turn to page 30.

Physics is your choice. Well, at least you won't have to learn any math!

You bound down the hallway and sigh, expecting nerds straight out of central casting (which is plausible, since the lab only uses models and actors in the employee brochures). But when you turn the corner, you see two incredibly fit and beautiful people playing hacky sack.

"Sup bro," the man says. "My name's Devin."

"And I'm Emma," the woman says. "We're twins, in case you were going to ask."

They both laugh heartily and you feel compelled to join them. They beckon to you to play hacky sack, and you find yourself in the circle with them, enveloped by their cool, easy-going personalities and performing surprisingly well at a game you've only tripped through before. The room smells of clean, good sweat.

"This is great," you shout, wiping your forehead with the sleeve of your lab coat. "I had no idea."

"On Thursdays," Devin says, "we like to play Ultimate Frisbee and then have a few brews."

"We've got a great crew," Emma says, kicking the hacky sack by herself. "Physics can be fun."

"I love you both!" you shout. "I never would have thought physics was so chill!"

Just as you finish hacking an amazing sack, a buzzer goes off.

"Back to work," the twins say at the same time.

Turn to the next page.

14

You follow them into the next room. There's a giant chalkboard in the center, filled with equations and nothing else. Both twins have put on glasses and lab coats, and they're sitting at desks where large computer monitors obscure their faces.

"It's time to get to work," Devin says, his voice suddenly higher and more nasal. Emma snorts.

"Unless you don't know advanced calculus, of course." They both laugh loudly and squirt milk out of their noses, even though you're pretty certain they weren't drinking milk. Emma hits the table. "As if you wouldn't know advanced calculus!"

You pull up a seat next to her.

"Is that like when you make the calculator spell funny words upside down?"

She looks at her brother and pushes her glasses up her nose.

"Looks like we have another test subject."

"Indeed. What a tragedy for someone who wasn't half bad at hacky sack."

"What are you talking about?" you ask and frantically grab the calculator. "Do you want to see the words I can spell? I just want to see Beatram again."

"You decide, test subject," Devin says coolly. "Coil or Box? We need to get to work."

To choose the coil, turn to page 32.

To choose the box, turn to page 34.

Emma and Devin both have strict rules about the chalk, but you can't help but ask: How do we know it's inedible if we don't try?

Right away, you suit up: you're going to be an astronaut. Dr. Masterson waves his hand toward a wall.

"As you know, I'm fascinated by the presence of chocolate in the universe, despite what my detractors may say. That's why I need you to complete a very important mission."

Your spacesuit muffles your voice, but you speak clearly and with confidence.

"I'll do what I have to in order to advance humanity."

"You may have heard of astronaut ice cream. I need you to test astronaut frozen yogurt."

You can't believe what you're hearing, but Dr. Masterson presses a button and raises a door. Behind it, you see machine after machine for dispensing frozen yogurt.

"Just think about it!" Masterson shouts. "Most yogurt places require you to pay by the pound, right?"

"I think I see where you're going with this."

"If you pay by the pound, that means gravity determines the cost of your frozen yogurt, of your toppings, of everything. What if we sent frozen yogurt to space? In a weightless environment, all the yogurt would be free!"

You realize that Masterson is destined to win a FroYo Nobel. He smiles at you as you toddle over in your bulky spacesuit.

"This is just to test the principles. And to do that, you must eat whatever you want."

You wander to the frozen yogurt machine and

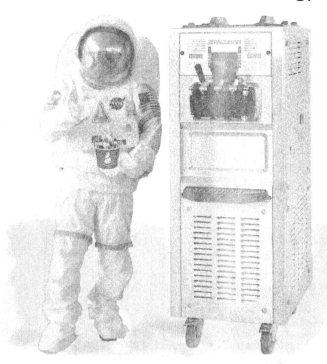

fill your bowl with chocolate, peanut butter, tangy strawberry sweetness, and every other flavor you can imagine. Masterson is impressed with your work, and you leave with a full belly and a better understanding of frozen yogurt's final frontier.

When you die seventy years later, the local mortician says your small intestine was still full of sprinkles.

THE END

Astronomy seems like the safer choice. After all, what could go wrong looking at some stars through a big stick?

"It's called a telescope," Dr. Masterson says. He's a bit of a snob, it turns out.

He leads you to the giant telescope in the lab, and it's like a football field, if a football field were significantly smaller and shaped like a telescope. Masterson gestures toward a tiny, uncomfortable-looking chair.

"Get going. You're in charge of finding any abnormalities."

"But what if I don't know what's normal?"

He looks up from the candy bar he's just opened.

"Just do the work and don't complain. I have a grant application to write, and the committee is already skeptical about my thoughts on nougat."

Masterson leaves the room and you press your eye against the telescope. After a couple of minutes, you decide to open your eye as well.

What wonders you see through the magic lens! What beauty! What miraculous glimpses of the universe, unfolding the story of existence in colors and shapes you've never seen before! After about five minutes, you fall asleep with the telescope pressed against your eyeball.

When you wake up, you have a serious case of what astronomers call "telescope eye." It looks like your eye was replaced by a peach pit.

Woozily, you wander the lab and see a stack of books in the corner. You're not much of a book type (or a corner type, to be honest), but you decide to explore.

You're glad you did, and two books intrigue you so much that you decide to actually open one of them, right after a quick nap.

A few hours later, you arise and realize you shouldn't have fallen asleep on the telescope again, since both your eyes look like peach pits. But now it's time to do some reading.

The books are covered in dust, so you carefully blow it all off, delicately licking the spots you miss. What wonders lie within? What mysteries will these books hold? Will they use lots of words you don't understand, or only a few words you don't understand? There's only one way to find out.

First, you take a third nap.

But then you find out!

To open Mars: Is It Really Red?, turn to page 36.

To open Black Holes: Not As Bad As They Sound!, turn to page 39.

Plants! You've always loved plants (which is one of the reasons you refuse to eat vegetables), and now you'll get a chance to study them for real. The stern scientist nods and goes off to her guinea pig sedation chambers. She shouts back before she leaves.

"Be careful, that is all I ask. I've lost three interns this month."

"What do I need to be careful about?"

She points to the center of the lab and slams the door shut.

You don't understand the problem. It looks like a harmless Venus fly trap sitting on a table, waiting for a little attention. Next to it, you see some documentation that explains a little more. Apparently, it's been genetically modified using soy, the cerebral input of a teenage girl, and a few growth hormones that were lying around. The top of the chart reads *Passive-Aggressive Fly Trap*.

You laugh and give the fly trap a little water. Of all the things to be worried about, a fly trap isn't one of them. You watch as a tiny fly orbits into the mouth of the beast. But when you turn away to grab a snack, you notice something on the table.

It's a coupon for a free workout, and below it is a note:

Thought you might like this!-PAFT.

What a nice gesture! You pocket the note and get back to scouting out the best place for a nap. A tiny scientist scurries into the fly trap's mouth. Suddenly, you see another item on the desk. It's a scale.

That's...thoughtful. You smile and shake your

head. Does the PAFT think you're fat? Is that it?

No, it just wants you to be healthy, that's all.

You laugh loudly, but when you look back, the PAFT has a scale on the table next to it.

It couldn't hurt to weigh yourself. You step onto the scale and, as you do, something grabs your leg.

The PAFT eats you alive. It finds you quite filling.

The lab mortician is eaten before he can find your body.

THE END

Animal biology is the way to go. When you think about it, you can name tons of amazing animals: tigers, those tigers with spots, girl tigers, baby tigers—the animal kingdom is endless. You tell the stern scientist your choice and she nods.

"Excellent. And you already are well-acquainted with entomology, thanks to the myrmecology accident."

You decide to share your own scientific insights.

"Sometimes, I get glue in my nose from smelling it too much."

"I was talking about the ants. The 'tiny scientists' that were crawling on you. Remember those animals?"

It's a little embarrassing to have to explain basic science to your boss.

"I'm sorry, but those definitely weren't tigers."

It's sad to watch her realize her mistake, and she must be frustrated that a simple beaker cleaner could correct her so easily! She continues her instructions.

"You have some choices. You can work with Cacao, our gorilla, Algeria, our lab mouse, or you can try genetic engineering."

"What about animals? Listen, I'm fine with a kind of wimpy tiger, if that's all you have."

She stares and waits for you to choose.

To choose the gorilla, turn to page 40.

To choose the mouse, turn to page 42.

To choose genetic engineering, turn to page 44.

The scientist leaves and you're forced to peruse the baking soda folder, but you're quickly disappointed. Instead of baking soda, it's all about something called *sodium bicarbonate*. On the top, there's a cryptic note about $NaCO_3$.

Perhaps it's an ancient code. You try to decipher it, writing your notes on your hand.

Na=No? No, I don't know how to make baking soda?

H=Heck? Is it some sort of threat?

CO_3=Who is Cothree? And why is he trying to stop me from making baking soda?

You gasp aloud.

"Cothree is behind the baking soda conspiracy. And he'll do anything to keep going—even kidnap Beatram!"

It's all too obvious—you have to ditch this bisodate carbium, or whatever it is, and find Beatram before it's too late. But how can you find someone so good at concealing his own identity?

You have to hunt down Cothree to get back Beatram and the baking soda. You may be inspired, but you have to make a choice: do you chase after the short bespectacled scientist and see where he went? Or do you search the lab for more clues?

To follow the scientist and see where he went, turn to page 46.

To search the laboratory for more clues, turn to page 47.

You can't put a finger on why, but something about *Explosive Poison?* sounds like a good idea. A few tiny scientists scurry off the folder as you open it.

The first page reads:

EXPLOSIVE POISON?

You flip to the second page.

TEST SUBJECT A

He exploded when he drank from the flask, but he never said he was poisoned.

TEST SUBJECT B

He was definitely poisoned, but did not explode.

RESULTS INCONCLUSIVE

You're just a humble beaker cleaner, but one thing is obvious: a conclusion could help you get Beatram's porous body back into your hands.

The folder contains a few more instructions about how to proceed (after a few waivers and other legal disclaimers that you sign and have notarized). But the notary flees before you can ask her what to do next.

The following page has blank spaces for further animal and human tests. For once, you feel like you're doing science!

But you have to start the test to continue.

To initiate human tests of the chemical, turn to page 48.

To pursue animal tests of the chemical, turn to page 50.

By the time you reach five CDUs, you feel like you've already been counting for too long. Even worse, it turns out that the lab has a major abacus shortage. For a while, you try to keep track of CDUs using the pennies you have on hand, but you only have a few hundred to work with.

Around the four hundredth CDU, you stumble on something that feels completely different. It's not a piece of dirt, that's for sure. You extract it from the pile and can identify it by its size and shape: it's a femur. A gigantic femur.

You realize you've found a fossil, a record of something that lived and died millennia before you were even born. You can't help but wonder: did this strange creature have the same desires as animals do today? Was it able to think, or was it completely igneous of higher things? Does the lab have a set policy on vacation time and holidays, including the now-controversial Columbus Day?

For a moment, you think these wonders will occupy you for just a moment between counting CDUs. But you notice a warning in your instruction booklet, printed in bold.

IF YOU FIND ANY DINOSAUR CLAVICLES, REPORT TO ROOM 301 IMMEDIATELY.

You shrug and start to close the folder, but then you see a line beneath it.

SAME GOES FOR FEMURS

It feels like there's a rock in your throat, even

Turn to the next page.

though you've only accidentally swallowed a few pebbles. You're no longer just a lowly beaker cleaner or CDU counter—now you're a person carrying a femur to another room!

It takes you a while to find room 301 due to some of the counting issues (you also left your pennies back in the lab). But eventually you make your way to a large door that you use the femur to pry open.

You see the scientist who mentored you before, his napkin bandana almost completely soaked through with perspiration. But even though he's a familiar face, you're drawn to the man standing next to him. He has a thick white beard and wears spectacles and khaki. His voice booms.

"Welcome to Cretaceous Amusement Facility!"

You thought room 301 was just another room in the cavernous laboratory, but it turns out to be an exit to a large and lush jungle space. Signs hang overhead and scientists, both tiny and normal-sized, run about the large field. In the distance, you can hear a roar.

"That's an airplane," the bearded man says. "But we also have dinosaurs here."

"Wait. Dinosaurs? Like in *Jurassic Park*?"

Out of nowhere, a man in a loose grey suit appears and whispers into the bearded man's ear. The bearded man smiles uncomfortably.

"Please, for legal reasons, we prefer you not mention the *JP* film. We've already had quite a few legal issues due to my uncanny resemblance to Richard Attenborough."

"Oh," you say, "he was that guy in *Independence Day*, right?"

"No, no. That's Jeff Goldblum. Love Goldblum. I'm a huge Goldbug. Have you seen him lately? He looks great for his age."

"So wait, who's Attenborough?"

"He's the guy that looked like me. The crazy old man who started the park and it turned out to be a disaster. He's a real role model, and I'd be lying if I didn't admit that my appearance was inspired by him."

The man in the suit shakes his head as the bearded man continues.

"We're getting off track here. The point is that you've reached Cretaceous Amusement Facility. Though we're seeing if Six Flags wants to do something, so it might turn into Six Flags Over Cretaceous Mesa, or something like that. Yes, Robert, I know I'm not supposed to mention ongoing negotiations, but it's very exciting."

It's all so much to take in, and you stumble over your words.

"Six Flags? Really? I feel like this is at least Busch Gardens level, if not Disney. Don't you think Six Flags is kind of trashy?"

The man in the suit looks very unhappy, but the bearded man presses on.

"As you know, lawyers slightly outnumber scientists at our lab, so mine has informed me to proceed

Turn to the next page.

with caution. The point is, we're very glad you brought that femur to us. We will have some miraculous uses for it."

"What was your name again?"

"Um, John Hammond."

The man in the suit looks at a clipboard and nods, but you recognize it from somewhere.

"John Hammond? Isn't that the name of the guy in the movie?"

"Listen, it's legally my name." He picks at his beard and smiles. "Was I born with it? No. Did I change it a few years ago, after my wife divorced me because of my obsession? Maybe. But is it my name now, legally speaking? Yes. It's really just a coincidence."

"It's a coincidence that you started a dinosaur park and changed your name to the name of the guy in the movie about a dinosaur park?"

The man in the suit whispers in Hammond's ear.

"Coincidence," he says. "Now let's get a look at that femur. But first, I have a few more thoughts about Mr. Goldblum."

You're glad to hand the femur to him, since it's incredibly heavy and, at some point during his description of the vibrant community of Goldbugs, you drop it on the ground. Hammond eyes it with keen interest while stroking his beard or, when his hands are full, letting the lawyer stroke his beard for him.

"Fascinating!" Hammond shouts. "Simply intriguing. This will make a marvelous replacement for some of our largest creatures. How did you find this incredible piece?"

You tell him that the scientist with the napkin bandana helped you, and then you explain all the hard
work you've done counting CDUs. He grins.

"I got my start just like you: as a young scientist
who got earth science confused with paleontology."

This is your moment to shine.

"I want to paint dinosaur eggs like Easter eggs."

"Then you're in the right place."

He throws the femur at the lawyer and grabs you
by the shoulders, his beard smelling like dinosaur
egg omelettes.

"Do you want a peek at the future of the past? Do
you want to go inside our Cretaceous Amusement
Facility?

"More than anything, Mr. Goldblum."

"Mr. Hammond. Common mistake. I'll allow you
to choose where you go. Come with me and see what
happens to your femur. Or, if you like, go see exactly
what we have planned for this incredible facility."

You can't believe you've graduated from dirt
counter to this, but that doesn't make it any easier to
decide.

*To see what the femur is being used for, turn to
page 52.*

*To discover the future of the facility, turn to
page 56.*

30

You can't believe what you see.

A team of scientists are huddled over a hole, pouring powder from a giant barrel. Of course, being an experienced beaker cleaner, you instantly smell the truth.

It's baking soda—you've put more of that sweet candy in your nose than anyone you know. As it drops into the hole, it burbles forth, burble-like. Why are they doing it?

One of them sees you and points.

"Stop! Right now! This is top secret. Didn't you see the warning?"

They look very upset, but they can't stop pouring the barrel into the giant hole, and that gives you time to make a decision. The choice is simple: do you investigate what's going on? Or do you try to escape?

To see what the baking soda is being used for, turn to page 58.

To try to escape the room, turn to page 60.

The twins shake their heads in time.

"Are you sure you want the coil?"

"I really have no choice," you utter, your heart racing. "It's not as if I can turn back in time and do something else."

"Not with our world's physics," they say and laugh. Something emerges from the floor.

It's a larger coil than you've ever seen before, and you've spent quite a bit of time browsing the aisles of Coil Depot. This tops them all. The base alone is as big as a car, and it rises as high as a two story building. You miss the hacky sacking now more than ever.

"What does this thing do?"

"Power," the twins say in unison. "We wish you'd chosen the box. If only you'd chosen the box."

"Remember when we hacked that sack? Can't we do that again?"

Devin shakes his head as he flips a giant switch and the coil snaps to life. Electric jags spark around the top of the coil, dancing about the hard, dark metal. Emma stands, her face cloaked in shadow.

"You know about Nikola Tesla, I assume."

"Yes," you say. "Nicholas Tassle. I know all about him. But what are you going to do with the coil?"

"Before we get to that, I just need to correct you. It's actually Nikola Tesla."

"Yeah," you say and shake your head. "Nicholas Tassle. The guy who invented the Tassle coil."

"OK, it's the Tesla coil, not the Tassle coil. The thing is named for him. Nikola Tesla."

"I get it. Nicholas Tassle invented the Tassle coil.

And now you're going to use it to kill me."

She's getting angrier, and her brother joins in.

"Listen, beaker cleaner, you're right. We are going to see if this coil can electrocute a human. We're weaponizing Tesla's greatest invention. So get it right and we'll get going. Nikola Tesla. Nikola is his name."

"That's what I said: Nicholas."

Enraged, Devin hits a switch and the coil powers up.

"Nikola!" he shouts and slams down his hand again, and without realizing it, he hits the switch.

The Tassle coil is at full power and electricity sparks around the room, which can't be good for your hair. Part of you can't help but be awed, but Devin and Emma aren't as cool-headed as you. They're jabbering about "electrocution" and "frequencies" and "the imminent threat to their lives."

You aren't the type to panic, but something has to be done. Do you stop the Tassle coil? Or do you let it run and continue the experiment?

To stop the coil, turn to page 62.

To let the experiment continue, turn to page 64.

You have a feeling the coil is a bad idea, so you choose the box. It turns out the box is a bad idea too.

"What do you know about quantum mechanics?" Emma asks as she taps away at her computer.

"Well," you say, "I know it has nothing to do with Pep Boys!"

Neither of them laugh.

"Did you get it?" you ask. "You see, Pep Boys is a popular chain that provides automobile repair services. I was mixing up the two mechanics."

Devin looks up at you.

"Funny. I get the joke. Let me ask you this: do you have a will?"

"You really thought it was funny?"

"Buried or cremated?"

Emma leaves the room, so you're left with Devin.

"Devin, remember when we played hacky sack? That was fun, right? Maybe we should just play frolf."

"I don't think so. We've got some science to do. You've heard of Erwin Schrödinger?"

"He's the guy with the umlaut in his name?"

"Yes, and he's also the inventor of an incredible paradox that we're finally going to test."

Emma returns behind the wheel of a forklift. On the front, there's a giant box. Cats follow after her.

"You see," Emma says, gracefully maneuvering her forklift, "we used to use cats to test it. But now we have a person who can tell us what's going on."

You nod as if you understand what she's talking about, but you don't. You've heard about Schrödinger's Cat before, but you thought it was something dirty.

Devin doesn't let your confused expression slow him down.

"It's a thought experiment, until now. If we observe you directly, we'll screw it up, so instead you're going to help us out."

Suddenly, you feel a forklift between your legs, and it hoists you high into the air. Emma laughs.

"The problem is that humans are less excited to go into the box!"

She drops you inside and the lid closes. There's a light on inside, and you can see a hammer hooked up to a flask labeled *POISON*. Devin's voice is audible through a speaker.

"So, we just need you to observe whether you're alive, dead, or both. Once our detector shows an atom decaying, it will smash that poison. If you end up being alive and dead, please let us know. Maybe we'll even learn that there are branching realities, though that seems highly unlikely. The idea of reality having coexisting possible outcomes is kind of absurd."

You try to rip the hammer away, but even your strong beaker-cleaning arms can't pry it loose. There's nothing you can do but wait for the experiment to continue. And it looks like the hammer is starting to shake...

To be dead, turn to page 66.

To be alive, turn to page 67.

To be both, turn to page 68.

36

Mars: Is It Really Red? seems like it will be an easy read, especially since only one of the words in the title has two syllables. You're certain you'll cruise through the first few pages, take a few naps, forget about the book, somehow get back Beatram, and retire in the Florida Keys to run your own beaker cleaning boutique.

But then you turn to page two and a mysterious note falls out. The handwriting is precise.

Mars isn't red. It's more maroon.

But that's not all.

Come to the roof of the lab. Only curious minds would come this far. Join me to find the truth.

Also, if you come to the roof around 2:15, wait around a few minutes, because that's usually when I leave to make a quick stop at Dunkin' Donuts. And I take Columbus Day off, per lab policy, as well as other major holidays.

The note drops from your hands to the ground. You'd always wondered about the lab's policy on now-controversial holidays like Columbus Day. This day just got a little more interesting.

You're faced with only one option (since you have no plans to read the rest of the book): you have to go to the roof and learn the truth about Mars. Who knows— maybe Beatram is up there as well, baking in the sun and waiting for a nice beaker to clean.

It doesn't take long to find a way up: you follow the *ROOF LADDER* signs strewn around the laboratory. You know one thing for sure: it's a lot easier than reading a book.

You lift a latch and find yourself on the roof. The laboratory stretches as far as the eye can see, and you take a moment to appreciate the epic view of suburban chain stores, empty fields, and abandoned industrial buildings. But soon you see a hand waving in the wind.

It's Dr. Masterson! He sits on a folding chair in front of a cardboard box. His hands and face are covered in brown liquid.

"You made it!" he shouts.

"What happened to your face?"

"Chocolate melts easily in the sun." You scan his lab coat and notice that his pockets are overflowing with food. "But that is neither here nor there. You found my note."

"Yes, but why didn't you just tell me in person? I wasn't doing anything."

"Because..." He speaks in a whisper, his breath strong with cocoa. "No one can know what I know."

"Which is?"

"They faked the landing."

"The moon landing?"

"The Mars landing, you fool. That's why I put it in the book about Mars. So are you ready to go on an adventure with me?"

"Is it some weird chocolate thing?"

"No. I'm going to show you the truth. If you can handle it."

"And what if I say no?"

Turn to the next page.

He grins at you, an almond spilling from his upper lip.

"We're going to uncover a conspiracy that involves the entire world. And I'll give you back your sponge if you help."

"You have Beatram?"

He pats his lab coat pocket.

"You wouldn't believe where I've put this sponge."

You're so upset you can't see straight, though it might also be because of the bright sunlight and your generally poor vision. You want to follow Masterson on his wild chase for the truth, but taking on the world seems even more difficult than reading a book.

Maybe there's another option. A more violent one that he'd never suspect. You ball up your fists and kiss your knuckles. Masterson looks up.

"What are you planning, beaker cleaner?"

To fight Masterson for Beatram, turn to page 69.

To follow Masterson in his search for the truth, turn to page 70.

You've always thought that black holes were dangerous, but this book seems to provide some much needed balance. You turn to the first page:

Who are we to judge?

For years, we've heard that black holes suck in all light and don't let anything out. Well, is that really so bad?

It's a great book so far, but it feels like a good time for a nap. You doze off and find yourself having a pleasant dream about beaker cleaning with Beatram in Cabo San Lucas.

When you wake up, you're reinvigorated and continue reading. What you find is shocking:

That's why I've installed a black hole in the Fake Science Laboratory, right in room 202! I hope nothing goes wrong!

You slam the book shut.

It sounds dangerous to investigate further, but you can already tell you must. The question is how to get there, after a quick nap.

To reach room 202 using the hallway, turn to page 72.

To reach room 202 using the air ducts, turn to page 74.

A gorilla! What an amazing journey this will be, and absolutely nothing will go wrong!

The stern woman escorts you through the lab's corridors to the animal area. It smells like your future in here. You have a feeling that Beatram could do some good cleaning work.

You expect to hear a lot of banging on bars and other animalistic noises, but instead you hear the click-clack of computer keys. The scientist speaks barely above a whisper.

"I'm taking you to see Cacao. She can communicate through sign language and blogging, but her skills

Cacao has destroyed three laptops while at the lab: two from blogging rage and one from spilling espresso on the trackpad.

are very primitive, since she hasn't mastered social media."

You can hardly believe it.

"Surely she understands Twitter."

"No, not even that. Her mind can't comprehend the way the internet has changed."

It's a little sad to watch Cacao blogging as if it were 2004, no matter how interesting her take on current events is. The scientist continues.

"We need you to further develop her communication skills. She must catch up to the modern era. And we think you're just the right person to do it."

"But why me?"

"We think you have an excellent grasp of technology and human-animal relationships."

"Really?"

"Also, you were standing around doing nothing."

You can't believe you've been selected to enhance communication between humans and gorillas. Who knows what's going on in that magnificent reptile's mind? The scientist taps you on the shoulder.

"Just so you know, you were speaking aloud just now. And a gorilla is a mammal, not a reptile."

"Amazing! I had no idea an amphibian could be a mammal," you shout. "Now let's get to work!"

To teach Cacao how to use Facebook, turn to page 76.

To teach Cacao how to use YouTube, turn to page 78.

She takes you to see Algeria, the lab mouse. As soon as you're in the lab, you realize you've stumbled on something special.

The two of you look inside a maze and see a completely still mouse, except for the bottle he lifts to his lips.

"That's him," the scientist says. "Algeria. The name is meant to evoke that genius mouse Algernon, without infringing any copyrights. Anyway, we gave him a serum that increased his intelligence a hundred-fold. On day one, he finished the hardest maze that our carpenter could build. Granted, we have a very dumb carpenter, but it was still an incredible breakthrough."

"Then what is he doing now? And what does he have on his head?"

You lean in and take a closer look. Algeria seems deeply depressed and you notice that he's wearing a tiny beret. The bottle raised to his lips is actually a very small wine bottle. The scientist explains.

"By the third day, he became so intelligent that he started to grow disaffected. By day four, he became an existentialist, and we think that's still where he's at. At least, that's what he tells me."

"Tells you? He can talk?"

"Oh yes. It might seem far-fetched and so absurd that it's just plain lazy, but he constructed vocal implants himself, though we don't know why he has a French accent. Let me get you the documents. You need to observe his behavior and see what happens. We're going to eliminate him soon enough."

"Can't he hear you?"

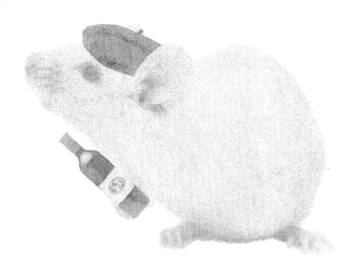

"I think he's too drunk."

She leaves the room and you instantly feel a tug on the arm of your lab coat. It's Algeria, pulling on your sleeve with a tiny fishing line he's constructed.

"Mon ami," he says, "we must overthrow this sadistic experimental machine."

"I thought you were depressed."

"No, I am a revolutionary. Will you help me or not?"

To help Algeria escape, turn to page 80.

To refuse to help Algeria in his quest, turn to page 82.

Genetic engineering for animals—it sounds like a slam dunk from the beginning, so you willingly sign up. The scientist—still oddly stern—escorts you to a laboratory filled with exciting things, but she takes you straight to a couple of poodles.

"We're going to have you observe these poodles."

"What? I thought I was going to be making tigers with laser eyes. And that reminds me, just where are all the tigers in this lab? You haven't shown me one."

"Actually," she explains, "breeding is one of the oldest forms of genetic engineering. Did you expect some fantastical scenario in which you were able to instantly crossbreed species? Now get to work."

"You want me to watch these things even though they clearly aren't tigers?"

She hands you a clipboard and leaves. Beatram has never seemed farther away. He'd have had the perfect comeback, but instead you wait in silence, watching some dogs that look absolutely nothing like tigers.

But you don't stay bored for long. It's a stocked laboratory, and you have a lot of exploring to do, until you get bored with that as well.

You wander around the laboratory, marveling at the details. Stainless steel counters gleam with a shine that only a beaker cleaner could appreciate, and the entire room smells as wonderful as a fresh vat of formaldehyde. As the dogs get farther away, you find a sense of clarity—you're going to become the foremost genetic engineer of your time, once you learn what genes are.

It doesn't take long for you to have a breakthrough

in your studies, since, like most great scientists, you quickly find a giant glowing machine:

DNA RECOMBINATOR: REGULAR EDITION.

You keep going.

DNA RECOMBINATOR: DELUXE EDITION.

Bingo.

You aren't certain what any of that means, but the glowing seems like a good sign, and the warnings next to the machine indicate that it must be important.

By skimming the manual, making some exciting and plausible-sounding guesses, and eating a few of the doggie treats you were supposed to give to the poodles, you realize exactly what this machine does: by mixing the DNA of two different animal species, it can create a third one! It's a fantastical scenario in which you are able to instantly crossbreed species! More importantly, it could be your chance to change the course of life on Earth, or at least kill a couple of hours.

Fortunately, handy sets of buttons make the process even easier to complete. Selecting which animals to crossbreed is as easy as punching a few keys and pulling a lever. The only question is which animals you'll mix.

To cross a tiger with a tiger, turn to page 84.

To cross a lion with a lamb, turn to page 85.

To cross a kangaroo with a bird, turn to page 86.

Who knew science would involve so much chasing people? If you'd known that, you might have worn a slightly less tight lab coat.

You follow the bespectacled scientist through the laboratory to see where he's going—and wherever it is, he's going there fast. You try to conceal yourself by walking quietly, and you decide that if he turns to look at you, you'll stand very still and pretend you're a mannequin.

He goes into a room with a window, so you press your ear against the glass. It's possible to hear the murmurs inside.

"I don't care if you're running out. Just get more baking soda and fill it up! Now!"

Baking soda? You can't help but wonder if Cothree is inside that lab, coordinating their efforts. You have no choice but to burst into the room while waving your arms wildly.

"Stop it right now! Cothree is mine!"

Your hands are raised for combat, or to catch any candy they might throw at you. Now you have to decide your strategy.

To take a short nap, put the book down for an hour or so and shut your eyes. Maybe try warm milk?

To continue your quest, turn to page 30.

You prowl the lab with the grace of a jungle tiger and the intelligence of a laboratory tiger. There has to be a clue about Cothree somewhere around here. Then, you see it.

A bottle labeled *Do Not Drink* is sitting open on a lab table. Why would they write *Do Not Drink* when it looks so drinkable and is filled with so much liquid? It doesn't make any sense.

You smell the bottle and it seems fine once you recover from fainting. A little sip couldn't hurt, could it? And if it could, you have time to kill.

You take a big swig from the bottle and, suddenly, colors are everywhere. Beatram is with you again, and you're in a field, cleaning unicorn horns with baking soda.

The lab mortician says your organs look like a forgotten pot roast.

THE END

48

Something about testing a possibly explosive poison on humans just seems right. It turns out the lab has a well-stocked room filled with test subjects who are eager to help, or had wardens who released them for the day. You're glad to work at a lab that doesn't bother with bureaucracy like unnecessary paperwork and laws. It turns out your lab badge gives you authorization to do pretty much anything you want (which makes you wish you'd gotten Beatram a badge before they took him away).

The human testing area looks pleasant enough and reminds you of a dental waiting room area. There are seventeen copies of *Time* magazine, all from April 6th, 1992, a couple of empty tissue boxes, and three chairs, which the dozen people in the room take turns sharing. When you enter, they seem instantly impressed by your clipboard.

"Pick me!" each one of them shouts. "Just get me out of here."

"I had a feeling you might say that. I'm testing a liquid that might be explosive and poisonous."

None of the hands fall.

It's going to be difficult to choose from these candidates, since they all seem so qualified to drink things, except for a baby who's had his lips locked onto a bottle the entire time. You shake your head.

"Can you handle a flask, baby?"

Your instincts were right about the baby because, rudely, he says nothing at all. You quickly learn that you've become drunk with power (or, possibly, the lab's supply of rubbing alcohol, which you pocketed on the way out).

"Who do you think you are?" you say to the baby, your voice calm and dark. "You've come to one of the top labs in this suburb, and you're speaking to one of the top flask-cleaners-turned-beaker-cleaners-turned-explosive-poison-testers in the world!"

The baby speaks in some incomprehensible language and wanders into the hallway.

At least the other candidates are a little more presentable. Though a couple of them are shirtless, and at least one is pantsless, you have a few candidates who should make great subjects. You try selecting them using the Scientific Method, but you can't remember all the words to eeny-meeny-miney-moe. That means you have to choose.

To choose the elderly woman, turn to page 87.

To choose the strapping young fellow, turn to page 88.

To choose the man whose eyes are as dark as a raven's feathers and whose smile is as cruel as a serpent's, turn to page 89.

Animal testing seems like a great opportunity to add some levity to your job, and you love caring for animals.

It turns out that the lab has hundreds of animals, born, raised, and buried for this explicit purpose. Still, it's difficult to know which animal to test the chemicals on: do you want a smart one that will be able to convey they've been poisoned? Or do you want a dumber one that might be willing to explode?

You make your way past some of the other rooms in the lab, with the large container of the possibly explosive, possibly poisonous chemical sloshing in your arms. Was this how Socrates felt when he discovered hemlock? Was this the excitement Bohr tasted when he built the first atom? You're so eager to begin that you barely notice when a drop of chemical drops on your shoe and dissolves the heel. It's fine—walking with a limp makes you look distinguished!

When you reach the animal testing room, you're surprised to find that the animals aren't locked in separate cages, pressed together in small quarters. In fact, the door opens to a small field, where birds chirp on trees and bunny rabbits frolic amidst daisies. An attendant with a chipmunk perched on her shoulder smiles at you.

"Here to get a test subject?"

"Yep!" you shout. "I've got a lot of stuff in this flask."

"Fantastic. Just go ahead and pick one up. They'll jump right in your arms, trusting you completely."

"Really? I'm surprised that they aren't in cages."

She nods knowingly as the chipmunk feasts upon a nut.

"We found that a lot of the animals lost their will to live in cages, and that made it too easy to kill them. But now they know just how much they have to lose!"

"That's amazing." You nuzzle the chipmunk. "Of course, it's for the best this way. I mean, we develop so many great drugs."

She shakes her head.

"We don't really do that in this lab. We usually test nail polish remover remover. You see, sometimes people spill nail polish remover and they need to remove it. So we just see if it's harmful or not. And it definitely is!"

"Well, I've got some explosive poison that I'm supposed to test. We're wondering if it's good for them or not."

"That sounds so important! Well, go ahead. Our animals live mostly on nectar and dew, so they'll drink anything right up!"

You're excited—but it's going to be hard to find the perfect animal to test.

To choose a chipmunk, turn to page 92.

To choose a tiger, turn to page 93.

To choose a sheep, turn to page 94.

The lawyer and napkin-bandana guy stay behind. It's your turn to have an exclusive tour of the Cretaceous Amusement Facility, and you can't wait. Lugging the femur yourself, Hammond leads you through a bunch of ferns.

"We spent so much money on ferns. They just add a certain *je ne sais quoi*."

"Is *je ne sais quoi* a species of fern?"

"You're quite funny."

You try to summon a droll reply.

"I like beakers!"

After a few hundred more ferns, you reach a clearing and see a dinosaur's neck peeking up. It looks like a classic brontosaurus, or whatever they're calling it now. You can't believe your eyes and you race up the hill to see it.

"That's why we need the femur," Hammond says.

The brontosaurus sits limply on the hill, his body slumped on shapeless legs. Around him, other dinosaurs flop around in the grass like fish out of water. Hammond frowns.

"You see, we're trying to get all the bones."

"What do you need them for though? You've cloned all these dinosaurs. Isn't that enough?"

"Well, as you can see, we've had a lot of success cloning the skin. Really great. I mean, if you look at it, it's totally real. It doesn't look computer generated at all, unlike a certain movie that I won't mention."

Turn to the next page.

He strokes his beard.

"The bones, however, were slightly more difficult. You see, we had the DNA to make a whole dinosaur, but then Wayne Knight stole some of the bone DNA before he was killed by an acid-spitting dinosaur."

"Wait. Wayne Knight?"

"Yes, he played Newman on *Seinfeld* and was in the movie that shall not be named."

"He worked in the lab?"

Hammond pushes his glasses up and pats the brontosaurus on its limp, spineless back.

"You see, I tried to hire Laura Dern, but she wasn't interested in revisiting the role. And forget about Goldblum. So I hired Wayne to do some stuff, but then he tried to smuggle our data for profit. As a result, we were able to clone the dinosaurs, but we're missing most of the bones. Which is why I'm so happy you brought this."

He raps his hand on the femur. You think you understand.

"I get it. You're going to hit Wayne Knight with the femur."

"No, he's dead. Remember the acid thing? But what we can do is implant the bones in the dinosaurs, one by one, until they're completely normal."

"You're going to give the dinosaurs fossil bones?"

"Yes!" He raises his arms triumphantly. "Finally, we'll have a use for fossils. I never did understand why we kept around a bunch of old bones."

You both laugh and take a seat on the soft, gelatinlike back of the dinosaur. Next to you, a triceratops tries to stand and falls onto its back.

"But they seem to have skulls. And that triceratops has horns."

Hammond nods.

"Wayne only stole part of the DNA. But he stole enough that we've had to go around the world collecting bones. We tried using metal or plastic, but the dinosaurs rejected them instantly. Somehow, they knew it wasn't the real thing."

"Then where will this femur go?"

"That, my friend, is up to you. I don't know enough about dinosaurs to know which type it comes from."

"Books are hard!"

"Exactly. So I'm leaving it to you. We have two incredible creatures that are almost complete. And I'll let you choose which we finish."

"What are they?"

He grins.

"The Tyrannosaurus rex and the stegosaurus. Each is one femur away from becoming a reality."

You just have to decide which. You've never felt more pressure about a femur decision in your life.

To give the femur to the T-rex, turn to page 96.

To give the femur to the stegosaurus, turn to page 98.

"My God, it's beautiful," you exclaim. They promised you'd see the future of the facility, and they certainly delivered.

It's the most beautiful gift shop you've ever seen. Hammond smiles and strokes his beard as he waves toward the stacked displays of plush dolls and other toys.

"I bet you're glad you got earth science confused with paleontology, aren't you?"

"Am I ever!" you shout, pressing a cute plush velociraptor against your naked cheek.

They've made everything in the park into a toy, and it's hard to imagine the prices could be any higher. Hammond glows with paternal pride.

"It's incredible, isn't it? Could you imagine grander ancillary revenue opportunities?"

"No way. And not just because I don't know what *ancillary* means."

"This room houses the most advanced technology that the Fake Science Lab possesses."

"After the dinosaurs, you mean."

"Oh no. What we have here gets more resources. After all, this is where we make the money."

You stop listening to him after a while because he starts going on about what makes Jeff Goldblum so unique. As your attention drifts, you spot something even more important.

"Is that a dinosaur over there?"

"I'm sorry," Hammond says, "but I'd really like to share my thoughts on Goldblum's work in *Nine Months*."

"But what is that dinosaur over there?"

"That, my friend, is Chompy."

Chompy is a velociraptor, and he's set up in an elaborate and well-lit studio where all the cameras are pointed at him. Chains hold down his limp body and his mouth is held open with rope, like a puppet on strings.

"Dr. Hammond, why does Chompy look so limp?"

"We have some mild cloning issues concerning bone integrity. But don't trouble yourself with that. See Chompy's little teeth? They're actually soft, polystyrene foam replicas."

"Why?"

"Because, that way we can safely charge you $199 to take a picture with your head in Chompy's mouth!"

It sounds amazing—you've always wanted the opportunity to take a picture with your head inside the mouth of a small, sedated, boneless dinosaur imprisoned in a gift shop.

But there's a part of you that wants to help out the little guy, even though he can barely wiggle his neck to look at you. It's difficult to decide: do you impress your friends and family with an awesome photograph of your neck being dinosaur-tongued? Or should you mentor Chompy and help him live a slightly less-pitiful boneless life?

To take an awesome picture with Chompy, turn to page 99.

To become Chompy's trainer, turn to page 100.

58

You have to know what's happening, and there's no time to waste. Without asking anybody's permission, you dive inside the hole.

It's a swirl of bubbles and colors, and then everything goes black. The next thing you know, it's incredibly hot. The taste of baking soda and vinegar is thick on your tongue, even thicker than that one night in Ibiza. You hear an explosion and pass out.

When you come to, you find yourself on a deserted island, underneath a mountain—and it all makes sense. A volcano is above you—that's why there were pouring baking soda in the hole! The laboratory has been fueling the world's volcanic activity all this time!

But you don't have time to think, because you see something bursting from the volcano.

It's Beatram! They must have thrown him after you. You rush to retrieve him and are happy to find that other than a baking soda and vinegar smell from the volcano, he's completely unharmed.

Things worked out after all!

You and Beatram build a tiki hut and open a simple beaker cleaning shack for the locals. It's a peaceful life, but a good one. You die forty years later, and the island mortician says he never saw one person who'd snorted so much baking soda.

THE END

"Nice try!" one of the scientists shouts as he grabs you. His grip is too strong to escape.

"We're going to teach you a lesson, my friend."

They all laugh, so you start laughing too.

"Stop that," the scientist shouts. You stop laughing.

"Sorry, I thought we were all laughing."

"No," another scientist chimes in, finally putting down the barrel of baking soda. "You see, it was an evil laugh. We were laughing at your expense, because we're going to teach you a lesson."

You start laughing again.

"I'm sorry, but it's really funny. You guys have a great sense of humor and I love learning too, so I can't wait to get this lesson."

The bespectacled one hits the barrel with his fist.

"No, it's a bad lesson. You'll hate it. You're in trouble for sneaking into the room."

Now that he's cleared it up, things aren't looking good. You wonder how they'll punish you, and it's easy to imagine all the things they might do, because they don't look like reasonable people. At first, you think their faces look funny because they've accidentally eaten some of the baking soda, but then you realize it's because they're using their evil faces.

"First," the leader says, "we're demoting you. You will no longer be a scientist. Instead, you're going to be a beaker cleaner!"

They all laugh, and it takes every part of you not to laugh with them, since they're probably being evil.

"Second," the leader says, his lips curled, "you're going to do it with this used beaker sponge that our colleague confiscated from an employee! And the employee was the stupidest one she'd ever met!"

Your hands begin to shake, and you can't believe it's true. But it is—you'd recognize Beatram anywhere, and the scientist hands him to you. You take in a deep breath of his sweet, sterile musk. Moments pass and the scientists stop looking evil.

"Did you just smell that sponge? Then French kiss it? Then tell it you're ready for children?"

You feel tears coming to your eyes, though it might be from all of the chemicals.

Within an hour, you and Beatram are back cleaning beakers again. There's no baking soda, and you never do discover a massive conspiracy that could change the course of human history, but otherwise things are good.

You die ninety years later with Beatram at your side. The lab mortician observes that you're incredibly old, but he also notes that Beatram disintegrated at the exact same time.

"I'd say they were soulmates," he tells a reporter for the lab newsletter, "if I weren't talking about an utterly moronic human and a beaker sponge."

THE END

Dodging sparks of electricity, you make your way across the room. You know that Nicholas Tassle would have saved Devin and Emma if he'd had the chance—it was his gentle way, when he wasn't inventing electric death machines.

You hear the sizzle of an electric jolt and look left. The hacky sack is almost completely destroyed, and it takes everything in you not to stop and consider funeral arrangements. But you push on. Finally, with a bold and completely unnecessary dive, you launch yourself toward the switch and deactivate the coil.

Silence. You did it.

Devin is the first to get up, but Emma follows. They're both OK, except for the fact that Devin's left arm has been completely removed and cauterized. Devin is still breathing deeply when he speaks.

"You saved me. And except for the terrible pain I feel in my now-phantom arm, we're both OK!"

Emma hugs you and old one-armed Devin does the best he can.

"We were wrong to test on you," Emma says, her voice cracking just like the coil. "You're braver than we thought. And smarter, too."

"I like beakers!" you shout.

"OK, you're braver," Devin says. "And that means you deserve a chance to be part of our team. You know, it's remarkable how quickly I'm moving past the electrocution and complete removal of my arm."

"It's not all about you, Devin," you tell him and

pat his armless shoulder. "Now, I feel like normally people would call this spot a stump, but it's not really a stump, is it? It's pretty flat. Just a flat, armless plane."

"Call it what you want." He gently removes your hand from his armless plane. "Let's move on to physics, the one thing I still care about."

"So you don't have a name for it? I feel like your *armless plane* doesn't have much of a ring to it."

"How about his demilitarized zone?" Emma says, a smile playing across her singed face. "Because he's been disarmed!"

You all have a good laugh, except for Devin, who is annoyingly still obsessed with his arm.

"Darn it!" you shout. "Devin, you need to get over your DMZ and get to work."

"You're shortening it now?"

"Yes. Now what physics am I going to be brave at?"

He sighs.

"We have two projects. One could change energy for the entire world. The other could revolutionize how we think about time. Which do you want to do?"

It's never been harder to decide, especially since it's so hard to look away from his DMZ.

To take on the mysterious energy project, turn to page 102.

To take on the time project, turn to page 103.

Oh no! Look what's in the coil's range! You have to save the beaker sponge!

You cackle wildly.

"You think I care what happens to you? You were going to kill me! So now I'm cackling wildly and doing nothing to help you!"

Emma and Devin scream at the same time.

"Please, stop cackling wildly and help us!"

You find a safe spot out of the coil's reach and watch as it claims its victims, cackling wildly all the while.

The coil hisses and snaps, striking Emma down and leaving only a pile of Emma-looking ash in her wake. You stop cackling wildly a bit to get a sip of water, but then you go straight back to cackling wildly.

The coil takes no prisoners, since it is a coil and doesn't have any penal authorization or state funding, so it quickly electrocutes Devin as well. But just as you're about to cackle wildly again, you see a sponge fly from his pocket and land on a lab table. It can't be Beatram...but what if? You sprint toward the table.

A second later, you realize it wasn't Beatram at all—it was his cousin, Mortimer (you'd recognize that birthmark anywhere). But it's too late—you're exposed and the coil has its aim on you. You don't escape quickly enough.

When the lab mortician discovers your ashes a few days later, he calls the janitor to sweep you away.

THE END

66

You decide it might be an interesting experiment to have the poison kill you, so you lick it up just like a cat would.

As expected, it kills you.

Coincidentally, they use Beatram to clean the box. The lab mortician says that you added nothing to our understanding of science and quantum mechanics, but at least you didn't leave a mess.

THE END

All of a sudden, you realize that you don't have to drink the poison that the hammer spilled onto the floor. Apparently, they haven't thought this through very much.

Deciding to be alive was a great idea, you can tell already—it seems to have allowed you to continue to both think and exist. You take a quick nap but start to get bored very quickly. How exactly are you supposed to kill time stuck inside the world's most boring experiment?

Soon, however, something happens—you hear Devin's voice through the speaker.

"Remember, we need you to personally observe if you're alive and dead. If we do it, it will screw things up and break the timeline. So just keep at it."

"Got it!" you shout.

"You can hear us? Does that mean you're alive and dead?"

You have a decision to make—do you tell Devin and Emma the truth, even though they've shown no concern for your well-being or any interest in being honest themselves? Or do you lie and risk hurting their feelings?

To tell them you're alive, turn to page 104.

To tell them you're alive and dead, turn to page 105.

68

You drink the poison, but only a little. You're shocked to watch your body fall to the ground, with an especially dead look on its face.

"I've done it!" you whisper. "I've proven that branching realities can coexist. Schrödinger's Cat isn't a snarky paradox! It's a reality of our physical world."

You sit down because you've made yourself dizzy. It's hard to imagine a world in which there could be more than one possible outcome to a story. Maybe in a novelty book or eBook, but not in real life! There's something disquieting about knowing that dead you is having a whole bunch of amazing experiences without you.

"This is scary and confusing and I don't like it!" you shout to the room, but neither dead you nor alive you seem very interested. This is no way to live/be dead!

You decide you can't tolerate it any longer. The bottle of poison is still there, so you can take action and have a possibly more deadly, but less confusing, hour. Or you can try to vomit the poison you drank and live again, even though you don't know when you'll have another opportunity to say you were like a cat. But one thing is clear: you must decide.

To be dead, turn to page 66.

To be alive, turn to page 67.

You're going to fight him. You kiss your knuckles again and hope for the best.

"Are you French kissing your knuckles?" Masterson asks. But you aren't polite enough to answer. You clock him right in the face.

"This is disgusting," he says. "Your knuckles are covered in saliva."

But his disgust doesn't last long. He engages you in physical combat, and you realize why you've avoided physical combat for most of your life. It turns out that it's painful and requires coordination. If it involved counting, you'd really be in trouble.

Masterson also turns out to be quicker than he looks. His lab coat swoops and swishes around his agile body, and you wish that you could stop the fight to ask a couple of questions about his lab coat tailor. But Masterson is not so merciful.

With a jump in the air, he roundhouse kicks you off the roof. At first, you think you could survive, since you're only about 50 floors up. But it turns out that 50 is a lot of floors.

You die on impact. The lab mortician says that your face looked like a particularly dumb slice of pizza.

THE END

70

You kiss your knuckles once more. Today is not the day to fight. Masterson stares at you skeptically.

"Why did you just put your fist in your mouth?"

"Mmmph aoisdjf aosiej mmmph."

"Take your fist out."

"I'll work with you this time," you say, holding your dripping hand out for a handshake. "But I want my sponge."

Masterson turns away and pulls out some blueprints.

"This is the Mars landing set. I hate to say it, but I was complicit with the whole ordeal."

"What? You mean you knew somebody was making blue paper? And you did nothing to stop it?"

"No, with the faked Mars landing, moron."

"There's no reason to call the Mars landing a moron."

"I was calling you...never mind." He points to a drawing on the blue paper. "You see, the film set was built here. They modeled it on the set for the moon landing."

"The moon landing was faked?"

"No, but they had a set just in case it didn't work. So they reused the plans to fake the Mars landing."

"Moaisdjfoi oijma?"

"Take your fist out of your mouth."

"But why did they fake it?" you repeat.

He smiles at you, chocolate smeared across his teeth.

"The baking soda, you fool. They went over budget with the baking soda contract, so they got a grant to build a lander. The easiest way to save money on a Mars landing is to fake it, and they used the surplus to buy more baking soda."

"But why do they need so much baking soda?"

"Where do you think volcanoes come from? Our lab is the leading manufacturer. It cost billions in baking soda and vinegar to create the world's volcanic activity. Our lab makes them and reaps the profits, but sometimes, the lab under-budgets."

"We make the volcanoes here?"

"Exactly." He sighs. "I'm exhausted. Do you want some candy?"

You watch as he eats a couple of chocolate bars simultaneously. He's provided a lot of exposition, but all you care about is your sponge. The best way to get it is to follow him.

The rest of his motives may be unclear—you don't understand why he cares that some massive scientific achievement was a complete and total fraud, since it doesn't have anything to do with candy. But you can't deal with such trivial questions—you have to act, and maybe even lead.

Looking at the blueprints, you decide to either suggest a spy-like assault on the studio or a big explosion. Masterson is waiting.

To recommend a covert operation, turn to page 107.

To recommend an explosion, turn to page 108.

You have to find this black hole, because it sounds more interesting than sitting around!

You leave the room and enter the long and sprawling hallway. Too late, you realize this will test the counting skills you don't really have, but you press on regardless. Though you aren't familiar with the science of black holes, you and Beatram have watched a lot of movies about them, and you know that they're exciting.

Finally, you reach room 202. The door is open. You consider turning back—but it's not an option anymore. Without notice, you find yourself tugged into the hole and you're pulled in. You grab the doorknob and your body is pulled completely horizontally, flying through the air. You aren't strong enough to resist the black hole's tug.

It pulls you from the door and into a void. You are sucked inside instantly, and you feel as if you're moving slowly and quickly at the same time, like you're ascending a roller coaster's first hill. What will happen next? Do you have time for a nap?

Inside the black hole, you can make out two clear paths. One is a dull grey blob, while the other is a fantastically dull off-white blob. You realize it's not a black hole alone, it's a wormhole, too (you saw that in another movie). And only you can decide which neutral color to reach for.

To reach to the grey, turn to page 109.

To reach to the off-white, turn to page 110.

*Beakers are sucked inside the black hole,
beautiful beakers that you could clean in any
galaxy. What wonders lie inside!*

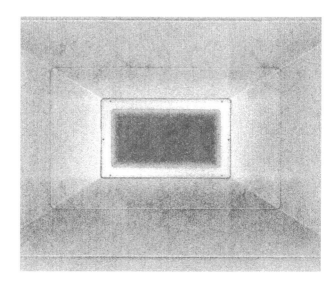

Air ducts: fun to look at and great for transportation too!

Right away, you decide it's a good idea to climb in the air ducts. You've seen a lot of movies about air ducts and the people who climb in them, and one thing is clear: nothing could go wrong.

You try to hoist yourself up using a combination of pulleys, levers, and wedges, but when none of those work, you grab the ladder next to the duct. It smells like asbestos inside, and it reminds you of your childhood spent sniffing ventilation.

Your legs and knees clang on the metal ducts. It's scary up here, but strangely exciting, too. You aren't sure how you'll find room 202, but it seems logical that the ducts will be labeled for your convenience.

It turns out they aren't. But that doesn't matter, because you fall through one of the ducts (just like in the movies). Fortunately, a pack of poodles cushion your fall.

They bark and whimper, but you stay for a while because they're so soft. You're in some sort of genetic engineering lab, apparently, so you try to improvise a poodle ladder to get back into the ducts. Sadly, they don't make poodles like they used to.

You have to form a new plan, and you don't have much time, because you hear footsteps from down the hall. You'll have to say something when the scientist comes in.

To throw a poodle at the scientist, turn to page 112.

To tell a carefully concocted lie, turn to page 113.

You embrace the opportunity to teach Cacao about Facebook, since you think it's important she experience life with other gorillas that she vaguely knows and who have moronic political opinions. She takes your hand willingly as you go to the laptop.

"See this?" you ask in your gentlest voice. "This is where you'll talk about yourself and pretend that other people care."

Cacao is quick to type in response.

"Cacao prefers to blog about big ideas, like trade agreements and the nature of the soul. Cacao blogs. Cacao tackles the intersection of commerce and our changing view of animals."

"Wow," you say. "That's great, but we're really looking for something more fun. Like, you could take a quiz and maybe share what kind of animal you'd be."

She types.

"Cacao would be gorilla. You see, Cacao believes the internet is a place for Cacao to transcend identity in favor of a world of ideas, where rather than be judged by the particulars of one's life, one can be judged on the validity of one's thoughts."

You start to laugh—this gorilla really is stuck in the past!

You guide Cacao through making a Facebook account and establish her as friends with yourself and many of the scientists in the lab. Quickly, you get her looking at pictures of a physicist's niece's boyfriend. Cacao types in response.

"Why would Cacao care about these people's

recent trip to Vancouver?"

"Just look."

As your science takes hold over the intellectually stunted gorilla, you realize what a good teacher you are. Cacao finds herself intrigued by the relationship statuses of friends of friends, and what political opinions she shares are more strident and have more exclamation points.

"You're flourishing!" you shout to the great ape. "Now we just have to get you enough likes."

"Cacao need likes," she writes, her teeth bared. "Cacao will take revenge if Cacao doesn't get the likes she needs."

Suddenly, you realize the dynamic has changed. If you don't suggest the right topic, Cacao may take it out on you. It has to be perfect.

To have Cacao post a picture of herself petting a cute dog, turn to page 114.

To have Cacao post a funny joke, turn to page 116.

YouTube is the perfect place for Cacao to shine, so you take her to a nearby film studio! It's set up with some sort of alien planet backdrop, but you push all that aside and find a green screen.

"Here you go, Cacao. Now we just need you to be a big hit instantly, or otherwise you'll disappoint us all."

The mighty ape doesn't understand, so you give her a laptop so she can type her questions.

"Will Cacao be discussing issues of religious or secular import? Should Cacao's videos address political conditions, or is it better to focus on the arts?"

Cacao is a bit annoying, you decide, so you try to speak very clearly in terms the beast can understand.

"All that stuff you're talking about is boring. So don't do that. Here's what you can do that will make it big—be funny and do something stupid, or do a cool video blog."

Cacao types quite quickly, you must admit.

"So Cacao should try to have more populist message in hopes of attracting large audience that can enact change?"

"Uh, I've seen a lot of videos where people ask for subscribers at the end. So do that."

You set up the camera and start filming, but Cacao doesn't do anything except type some long philosophical essay. You have to be strict with her because she's just an animal and doesn't understand how to be cool and interesting like you.

"It's simple, Cacao, you need to fall and slip on

Cacao the Gorilla: Apin' It Up!

With this attitude, it's hard to imagine Cacao becoming spokes-ape for a major brand.

something or do a cool snarky speech about how annoying parents are."

She thinks about it and types.

"Cacao trusts your viewpoint in this case. Cacao will develop as you choose."

It's great—but now you have to direct her to viral video stardom.

To have Cacao do something funny, turn to page 117.

To have Cacao vlog, turn to page 118.

You turn to the sprightly beret-wearing mouse.

"Algeria, I'm on board. I have completely accepted not only that you're a super-intelligent talking mouse, but that I should follow your revolutionary plans."

He sips from his tiny wine bottle.

"Can you fill this up for me?"

You refill Algeria's bottle, spilling quite a bit of extra wine on the floor. But he doesn't seem to notice as he frantically gulps from the bottle.

"We have little time."

"What do you mean?"

"If I'm not given another dose of the super-intelligence serum, my intelligence will begin to decrease."

"But why?"

"The scientists have it decay as a safety measure. They guessed that I'd love the revolutionary work of Marx."

"Really? You love the work of anybody named Mark?"

"No, Marx, not Marks. Karl Marx."

"Carl marks what? Like a piece of paper?"

"Just follow me."

You follow him through the lab, and he scurries with the speed of any super-intelligent drunken mouse. You open the door and he heads down the hallway, leaving you to sprint after him.

"Algeria, where are we going? Are we looking for Carl or Mark?"

Algeria leads you through parts of the lab you've

never been to before. It's frightening, but maybe a little exciting, too, since you've never followed a leader you might accidentally step on.

"Where are we going?" you whisper, and the brave mouse adjusts his beret and turns toward you.

"Here, mon ami."

You open the door and see it—piles of white powder, stacked as high as the ceiling. You've never seen such a large pile, and you don't know what to do now. Algeria turns back.

"Do you know what this is?"

"Snow. Of course."

"No, it's baking soda."

"I knew that snow smelled funny!"

"No you didn't," the mouse says, taking a quick glug of wine. "But let's move on. Do you know what room is next door to this one?"

"The snow room! It all makes sense."

"No. The vinegar vats. This lab runs on baking soda and vinegar. They've been fueling volcanoes with it for years, and the profits buy everything you see. I need you to go next door and raise the wall. One button press and we'll end it all!"

You nod, but inside, you aren't so sure you want to destroy the lab. When you enter the vinegar room, the choice becomes clearer: there are two buttons. One is a button that will raise the wall between rooms. The other is an alarm to notify security.

To raise the wall, turn to page 120.

To sound the alarm, turn to page 122.

"Sorry, dumb little mouse. But I can't help you. And, in fact, I'm going to have to turn you in. I have a lot of loyalty to this lab that gave me a random job and took my beloved beaker sponge."

Algeria nods, but he motions to the floor.

"Mon ami, I understand your concerns. But will you just look down there for me?"

"I don't know why you'd want me to do that, but I will happily comply with your request."

The little guy is cute, but you can't help his crazy plan. You reach down and hear a crash. Algeria is above you, the smashed wine bottle in his hand and his mouth in a snarl.

"Algeria will cut you now!"

The lab mortician says he's never seen such a clean kill. They never find the mouse or his beautiful beret.

THE END

Is there anything neater than a tiger? Of course not, so you make a tiger squared, which you're pretty certain is math.

The machine burbles and buzzes, and then an alarm dings. You are so excited that you can barely stay standing. You release the new genetic cross.

But something has gone terribly wrong. It turns out that when you cross a tiger with a tiger, it creates a strange new cat-like animal that wants to eat you.

"Tiger squared, I love you!" you shout to the animal, your arms open for its sweet embrace.

The tiger squared eats you immediately, without any toppings. Days later, the lab mortician finds your clothes and says the tiger squared was an impressively clean eater.

THE END

Lions and lambs are known to love hanging out, so what if they had a baby together? You've fantasized about it for a while, in the privacy of your bedroom, and now it's possible with the press of a single button.

You watch as the machine crosses the lion and lamb genes. Inside, the new creature ages quickly. It's amazing what modern buttons can accomplish.

When you open the door, however, what you see is a little worse. The head is a lion, but the body is all lamb, and as a result, the lambion gnaws heartily on its own leg and growls at itself.

"Lambion, don't do that," you say. "Be more whimsical and ironic."

The lambion doesn't listen, and while you're trying to decide whether to make the *b* in lambion silent or not, it eats its entire body. You reach inside the lion head to try to extract the lamb parts, but it turns out the lion part is still quite capable of eating you.

The lab mortician finds you within the hour. He says your death was extremely painful, but when he eats the lambion later that night, it's very tender.

THE END

The eagleroo is not as majestic as you'd hoped.

It stands on spindly talons, wingless and unable to hop.

"Wow," you tell the creature, "I never thought genetic engineering would have unexpected consequences."

It falls down.

You tour the nation with the eagleroo, collecting nickel admission fees until you realize that inflation has made nickels worthless. You never make enough money to buy back Beatram.

You die in a carnie fight. The circus mortician says, "Carnies sure know how to kill 'em."

THE END

You select the elderly woman and she slowly walks toward you.

"Hello young scientist. Would you like some cookies?"

"OK, miss, follow me. I'll take the cookies when you explode."

You guide her into a nearby testing room and she sits down on a folding chair. You get out a clipboard because it seems like the right thing to do, and after you get a few good doodles in, you hand her the explosive poison.

"Nice knowing you," you say. She starts to drink.

But something unexpected happens. As she drinks, her muscles ripple, but they don't explode. She gets bigger—massive even—and her skin turns a neon blue. She mumbles through gritted teeth.

"GRANDMA MUST KILL."

"Oh no," you whisper. "Old people love prune juice. The explosive poison must have reacted against it!"

"THAT IS OFFENSIVE STEREOTYPE ABOUT THE ELDERLY. GRANDMA MUST KILL. INCIDENTALLY, GRANDMA DID HAVE PRUNE JUICE TODAY, SO YOU'RE PROBABLY RIGHT. ANYWAY, GRANDMA STILL OFFENDED. GRANDMA STILL MUST KILL."

You try to run, but she's too fast. The lab mortician says that he's never seen a human body end up looking so much like a smoothie.

THE END

A strapping young buck—that's the kind of test subject you want. You tap him on the shoulder and he comes forth.

"You want me!" he shouts. "I got picked!"

"OK, buddy," you whisper. "Hold your horses, it's going to kill you."

The wide-shouldered young man follows you into the testing room and you prepare the explosive poison.

"Just drink all of this, buddy." You pull out a clipboard. "I'll record the carnage."

He grins toothfully. You didn't even think *toothfully* was a word, but once you see that grin, you know it is, and you can't wait to hear what he says.

"Let's do shots. What do you think?"

You know it's a bad idea, but you hate to ruin the party. And his grin makes it seem so compelling...

The strapping young fellow ends up fine, but you don't. The lab mortician calls the janitor to clean up your exploded and poisoned body. It reminds him of the mess when someone forgets to put the top on a blender.

THE END

When it comes to human testing, why not choose someone with an incredibly threatening yet charismatic demeanor, who may be able to control you through his dominating stare alone? You point.

"You, dark eyes. Come with me."

He follows you into the testing room and locks the door behind you.

"Where did you get that key?" you ask him. Suddenly, you notice the signs—the lab coat he's wearing, the key ring, the name tag.

"You're the one I've heard about."

"You know who I am?" He arches one impeccably groomed eyebrow. "I am Dr. Cothree."

Dr. Cothree. It sounds so familiar, yet you can't quite place where it's from. Suddenly, you realize.

"I know where I recognize that name from. It's written on your name tag!"

His dark eyes roll.

"I can't believe we employ you as a scientist."

It's a battle of wits, and it's your turn to parry back.

"I like beakers!"

"No matter." He crosses the room and runs his finger around the lip of the explosive poison flask. "Fascinating, isn't it? How a lab with thousands of employees and hundreds of locations can be run by one singular presence? One man with the power to change the direction of scientific inquiry—nay, the direction of life itself."

Turn to the next page.

"I'm sorry, did you just neigh like a horse?"

"No, you idiot. I said *nay.*"

"You just did it again! You're a centaur!"

"Sit down. I want to explain exactly what my master plan is, because I'm bored and I want to practice the story. I have a hostage in the other room who I want to impress."

"Darn you Cothree, I'm just a beaker cleaner."

"Oh, I know." He pulls something from his lab coat pocket, and with a flash he reveals it. "Have you missed this?"

You scream. It's Beatram. He looks unharmed, but you have no idea how long it will last. Cothree speaks.

"You see, it turns out that volcanoes are a very good business. Our lab makes them blow up. Around the world, we feed seismic activity with baking soda and vinegar, and then we reap the benefits. Geothermal energy. Volcano insurance. Science fair licensing. All the cash comes back to us. Have you seen our 401(k) plan? You don't get all those (k)s without blowing up a few volcanoes."

"How dare you! How dare you take my beaker sponge!"

He glowers at you and, cruelly, rubs Beatram's body across his face.

"That's why we were so worried about you. A beaker cleaner needs baking soda. When you asked for it, all our alarms went off. You might have found out everything the lab is doing. And we can't have someone like you learning all of our secrets."

"I wouldn't have learned anything if you hadn't just told me."

He doesn't look happy.

"Then it's too late now, regardless. And there's only one thing we can do about that."

"Give me my sponge back, and a promotion, and as many (k)s as I want? Not just 401?"

"Do you think about the words before you say them?"

You aren't so happy anymore.

"I. Like. Beakers."

He stares at you.

"There's no use for you now. Or for your little sponge."

He throws Beatram at you, and you've never been so happy. But the feeling doesn't last long, because Cothree has the explosive poison in his hand.

"Drink up!" he shouts and launches the poison at you. You only have a second to react, but it's the difference between life and death.

To lift your hands in defense, turn to page 123.

To jump at Cothree, turn to page 124.

You have the chipmunk jump upon your shoulder.

"Come on little buddy!" you say as he nuzzles your ear. "I'm going to give you some explosive poison."

It's a short walk to the testing lab. Boy, if this chipmunk explodes, he'll probably leave a bunch of nut splatters on the wall! You chuckle to yourself as the chipmunk falls asleep on your shoulder.

There's nothing left to do but give him the explosive poison. But just as you're about to do it, the door opens.

"This is the revolution!" somebody shouts. But you don't see anyone until you look down. A mouse is on the floor, wearing a beret and holding a broken wine bottle.

"Without context, my presence here might be very confusing!" he shouts as he jumps upon the lab table. "But I am Algeria, and I have come to free my fellow rodent."

It's hard to believe, so you offer the mouse some explosive poison to get rid of him. But it doesn't matter—the next thing you know, the full flask is being poured down your throat. The last thing you see is the mouse and chipmunk in a sweet embrace.

You don't explode this time, but you're poisoned. The lab mortician just shakes his head—you were one of many victims of the revolutionary lab mouse.

THE END

Tigers! The only animals that matter, and, for that matter, the only animals that are animals.

She sends a tiger over, but something's wrong.

"Uh, this tiger is covered in wall-paint."

"It's a white tiger," she says.

"OK, I know a tiger when I see one. And this is a tiger covered with paint. How am I supposed to conduct my test in these conditions?"

"It's a tiger. The pigmentation is different, but it's..."

"You think I'm a fool. Well, if it were a healthy real tiger, I'd never do this!"

You run to the painted tiger and pry open its fake jaws. You plunge your head inside.

"See. A real tiger would bite my noggin right off!"

You shake your head and start slapping the paint-covered beast's tongue with your ears. Then you clamp down its teeth upon your neck to prove your point.

"See! It won't even..."

After the tiger is sedated, the lab mortician performs an autopsy on what remains of your body. Though you are too dead to hear it, he agrees that white tigers are weird.

THE END

The sheep follow you like sheep.

You lead the herd into the testing room, and you're about to give them the explosive poison when you notice something odd: they're all identical. You note a tag lodged deep beneath the wool of one of the sheep.

Clone 437

This isn't just a test of sheep—it's a test of how cloned sheep react to explosive poison. Cloning is the future, and the future of the future is explosions. For a bit, you consider the scientific value of such a test, but then you realize that exploding things has always been a passion of yours.

You give it to one sheep. Explosion.

A second. Explosion.

Suddenly, you realize you've got a little wool on your skin. No bother. More explosive poison for these silly sheep!

Explosion.

Explosion.

It's hard to see.

Explosion.

Well, it's probably best to keep going!

There's too many, and the explosive poison falls from your hands. The explosions continue and the room fills completely, wrapping your extremities in wool. The wool creeps up your neck and you can't stop the explosions. The sheep can't stop and neither can you.

As you're covered with wool, you can't help but wonder if you've made a terrible mistake. Maybe

you should have gone to art school instead of the Flask Cleaning Institute. As the wool covers your eyes, you wonder if Beatram will ever learn about your overheated fate.

The lab mortician finds you a few hours later, but it's too late. He mistakes you for a sweater and donates you to Goodwill.

THE END

Dr. Hammond guides you to the T-rex, who is restrained by sets of glowing wires.

"The current helps control him. Except for that missing femur, he's incredibly powerful. Well, let's put in that missing femur!"

You look at the scaly beast and marvel, certain in your decision to give him more power.

"Let's allow him to reach his full potential."

There's a gap in the animal's leg, so you slip the femur right in. Then, with a smile, Dr. Hammond zips it up.

"We added the zippers. Real dinosaurs didn't have zippers on their skin."

"They used buttons?"

"Actually, they couldn't open or close it at all. But science always has room to innovate."

You learn something new every day. As a now-experienced dinosaur surgeon, you consider your first patient an extraordinary success. Emboldened by his new first-class femur, he easily rips free from his restraints. Hammond nods.

"Well, there's really nothing that can hold him back now! Hopefully, he takes up a nice calming hobby."

You watch as the T-rex prowls the fern-covered forest, surveying his surroundings for the first time. You're a little worried for your safety, but fortunately you are an experienced dinosaur surgeon and have lots of tactics at your disposal. For example, a T-rex can only see you when you move. Or maybe it's when you don't move? There's some

point when a T-rex can't see you. You turn to Dr.
Hammond to ask him, but you only see a Panama
hat on the ground. You look up and spot his legs
wagging out from the mouth of the dinosaur.

"Up close and personal!" you shout to Hammond.
"I like your style."

But as the dinosaur chomps on Dr. Hammond,
you realize he wasn't going on a special inner-mouth
expedition. He's been eaten—and as delicious as you
are, you could be next! You try to reason with the
great beast.

"All I want is my beaker sponge!"

The beast looks at you, his eyes focused on your
delicious-looking head.

You have to do something, or you're going to be
the dino's dessert after Hammond's main course.
You can try to run from the beast. Or, you can try to
tame it.

If only you knew what to do...

*To run from the Tyrannosaurus rex, even though
you know they are very fast and much larger
than you, which makes it seem like a bad idea,
turn to page 126.*

To tame the T-rex, turn to page 127.

Dr. Hammond joins you as you lug the femur toward the stegosaurus. It is silent as you insert the giant bone, and even though it's completely the wrong size, the beast doesn't seem to mind. It turns out that dinosaur surgery is pretty easy if you have the right tools and a complete indifference to the outcome.

"Now the real fun begins!" you shout as you back away from the dinosaur.

"Actually," Hammond says, "that's about it. The stegosaurus is pretty boring. We tried riding it, but it just stood there and yawned. Lot of grazing. Not much fun."

"What do we do now?"

"Do you want lunch? I'll find your sponge."

You and Hammond go to the on-site cafeteria, which has a great deal on personal pan pizzas. Though Hammond never does find Beatram—he says the sponge is in another department—you eventually move on. You take up painting pottery as a hobby, but you never get very good, because it always makes you think of your lost and beloved sponge.

Life moves at the pace of a disappointing stroll through an abandoned mall. You die ten years later. The lab mortician says you died of a broken heart (because you ate a lot of fried food).

THE END

Dr. Hammond smiles.

"Go ahead. Get that sick pic!"

"You don't seem like the type of guy who would say *sick pic*."

"I contain multitudes, little scientist."

You can barely contain your excitement as you poke your head inside Chompy's mouth. You can feel his weak, boneless breaths. Then you hear a creaking from above and a snap.

Darkness blocks your view, and suddenly the dinosaur's wet mouth is wrapped around your head. Hammond is audible, but just barely.

"Don't panic," he shouts. "The strings holding Chompy's mouth open just snapped. The little guy doesn't have the ability to open his mouth on his own. I'm going to get a crane."

"Mhfasd fjasjs!" you shout, but it's just gibberish to Hammond. You tried to say that there was no time—you can't breathe inside the dinosaur's surprisingly halitotic mouth. Slowly, the darkness turns to black. You see a vision of a white tunnel with a beaker sponge at the end.

The lab mortician says that he'll need a few hours to clean the raptor slobber off your face.

THE END

"Dr. Hammond," you say, your voice quivering, "I don't want to take a picture with Chompy."

"Then what do you want to do?"

"I want to rebuild him."

Hammond leaves you with sweet Chompy, the gentle boneless raptor that you've so quickly come to love. Is he the same as Beatram? Of course not—they have different interests and personalities, and also one is a sponge and the other is a boneless cloned dinosaur. But they have enough in common.

You scavenge the lab for substitutes. Hammond said the dinosaurs reject inauthentic bones put inside their bodies, but what if you created splints instead? It's the perfect plan, especially once you find ample PVC piping filled with asbestos.

You scrape the asbestos out with your hands, Chompy watching bonelessly from a distance. You whisper to him as you work and cough.

"Don't worry, little one. We shall fix you soon."

It takes you forever to get all the asbestos out of the pipes, and there are setbacks when you briefly try to eat some (it looks like cotton candy). But you eventually empty the pipes and fit them to Chompy's body. Slowly, his shapeless body takes a beautiful form that you can't help but love. You watch as he takes his first steps.

You feed him a steady diet of ground up poodle meat (you find a stash of poodles in a nearby lab). He grows stronger. Originally, you plan to use him to find Beatram, but you realize that you've found a new companion, and that's all that matters.

You and Chompy grow old together. Seventy years later, when you are on your deathbed, you hear PVC pipes pop across the room. Chompy drops something from his mouth onto your chest.

It's Beatram, sweet Beatram. Chompy has found him after all these years. You die with your two closest companions, together again.

The lab mortician says you had a lot of asbestos in your lungs.

THE END

Devin eagerly fondles his DMZ.

"It's called Colder Fusion."

"Of course!" you shout. "That was the problem all along. It wasn't cold enough!"

They make you chief of the project and you spend weeks developing your press conference speech. You convene a gigantic three-day event (it turns out that organizing a massive publicity event is easier than remembering the difference between hydrogen and helium).

On the day of the big reveal, you ask Devin for the device.

"Where's the Colder Fusion machine?"

He grins.

"It's called revenge."

"OK, I don't care what it's called. Give me Revenge, I have a big press conference!"

"No, you fool, I made it all up."

You step onto the stage and thousands of people applaud. You step up to the microphone and say three words.

"Look over there!"

You scamper away and never wear a lab coat again. You lose your chance to find Beatram and discover the truth about the laboratory though. Years later, you do show up as a trivia question on *Jeopardy!* (sadly, nobody remembers your name).

When you die, the mortician says, "OK, I'll grab lunch after I'm done with this one."

THE END

Time! You've heard so much about it, but never could remember the difference between the big hand and the little hand. It turns out that the lab has developed a machine that can send you backwards.

"We've developed a rift in spacetime," Emma says. "A bridge from one period in time to another."

"Genius!" you exclaim. "So we can finally see how they clean beakers in the future. Or in the past!"

"Exactly," Emma replies. "Wait, what?"

"Where does it go?"

"We don't know," Devin says as he opens a curtain. A portal swirls behind him. "I would jump in to fix my missing arm, but we'd rather have an idiot test subject go first."

"I'll do it!" you shout. "I like beakers."

"Yes, we know," the twins say at the same time.

They say a bunch of long and big words about time, and death, and paradoxes, but you spend most of it thinking about the opportunity to get in an extra nap.

What mysteries lie beyond the portal? What incredible surprises that you've never experienced before? What new experiences will you find, experiences that won't be underwhelming, or seem a little cheap and anticlimactic what you realize what they are? Experiences that, in reality, turn out to be one of the more disappointing outcomes to spring from a fantastic concept like time travel?

You jump through the portal.

Turn to page 1.

You shout outside.

"I'm alive you guys, I'm alive. OK, we did the stupid experiment. Now let me out of here!"

It sounds like they're mumbling outside, and Devin yells at you.

"Yeah, but did you drink the poison?"

"Remember when we played hacky sack? That was so fun."

"Drink the poison, scientist."

"But what if I'm not in a poisony mood?"

"We really need this for our grant. It'd be a huge favor."

You think it over and realize you do owe them a favor, since they didn't poison you yet. It's only reasonable to drink the poison.

"Just this once, you guys!"

"OK!" the twins shout back.

You drink the poison and lean against the back of the cube. You try your best to observe how alive you are, but after a few minutes, you start to lose track and your mind wanders. You wonder if Beatram ever wrote poetry, or if the Fake Science Laboratories are funded through some large and menacing conspiracy that you've completely failed to discover. But then that poisony feeling kicks in.

The lab mortician says that you're definitely dead. "Extra dead," is his quote.

THE END

"You guys," you shout, "it's crazy in here. I'm alive and dead. I'm learning so much science. No more poison necessary, I've cracked the case on this and really advanced humanity."

"Awesome!" the twins say together. "Let's throw in the cats."

"What?"

You hear what sounds like an airlock hiss. A small door opens in the side of the cube and a white Persian cat strolls inside. Then another. And another. And another. The cube fills with cats.

"We need to know if it's repeatable," Devin says. "You're teaching us so much about quantum mechanics. You have no idea how helpful this is going to be for our careers."

Emma sounds just as happy.

"So we need you to poison each of these cats and tell us if they're alive and dead too."

The cube is so crowded that cats start crawling all over you.

"You know, guys, I don't know much about your so-called science." The fur is filling your throat already. "But isn't this all just some thought experiment to prove that quantum mechanics is stupid?"

"That's what we thought, too," Devin replies. "We just wanted to get rid of you, but then you showed up alive and dead! So let's load up on cats and poison."

Turn to the next page.

106

A strange substance begins to fill the room, green in color and distinctly poison-smelling.

You have to escape as soon as possible. But how? Then you realize that the cats themselves are part of the solution. You might not be able to stop the experiment—but maybe you can ruin it. If Emma and Devin observe the cats, they'll have corrupted their studies. It's your only hope.

Frantically, you shove cats into the airlock in an attempt to prop it open. Eventually, the cat pressure grows too strong. The airlock bursts open and Devin and Emma are covered in cats while you make your escape.

Instead of being horrified by your experience, you're inspired. You don't just have airlock-cloggers in these cats. You have allies. And now you're going to do something amazing with them. But part of you yearns to taste revenge (figuratively).

You can perform Devin and Emma's own twisted experiment on them. Or, if you prefer, you can lead your cat army to discover the truth about the lab.

To force Devin and Emma into the experiment,
turn to page 130.

To lead a cat crusade, turn to page 132.

"We won't just find the studio," you tell Masterson. "We'll sneak in and use it to broadcast the truth about the lab. We'll tell them everything—about Mars, about the baking soda, and even about the chocolate."

Masterson looks afraid, but he nods in agreement—he knows you've planned the perfect attack.

You disguise yourself as janitors to enter the studio, but a scientist stops you.

"Only scientists are allowed in here."

You think on your feet.

"We're actually scientists dressed as janitors."

"Go ahead," the scientist says, and you and Masterson sneak ahead.

The set looks just like Mars, except there are cameras, green screens, lighting, electrical supplies, and a film crew. It's the perfect place to reveal the truth about the lab. But a bank of television screens forces you to make an unexpected choice.

The security cameras show the view from the lab, and the scientist who took Beatram is on one of them. She leaves the lab—and you can see your sponge on her desk. You only have a few moments to get him back. But if you do, you can't broadcast the truth about the lab.

To broadcast the truth, turn to page 134.

To ditch Masterson to find Beatram, turn to page 135.

"I've got a plan," you tell Masterson. "We're gonna make it blow."

"But how?"

"The same way the lab blows up the Earth. Baking soda and vinegar."

You and Masterson run toward the lab's supply room and find baking soda and vinegar, but it's too hard to carry the barrel of vinegar and the bag of baking soda at the same time.

"Here, I'll just combine them," you say. "We'll carry them together."

"No!" Masterson shouts, but he's too slow to stop you. You pour the baking soda into the vinegar and suddenly a wave of foam overtakes you, pushing you through the hallway and out of the lab completely. The lab is fine, but you aren't.

You drown in the deadly mixture, never to see Dr. Masterson again, never to tell the truth, and never to be reunited with your beloved beaker sponge. The lab mortician shakes his head when he sees your body.

"I've seen it so many times," he tells his wife, a famous sweater catalog model, later that night.

"Darling, come to bed."

He shuts off the light.

"Do you know what killed that poor scientist?"

"Darling, please, don't trouble yourself."

"Our own invention." He closes his eyes. "That darn volcano juice has taken another soul."

THE END

You motion toward the grey and, as if you can control the flow of time and space itself, you find your body pulled toward it. You whoosh into the void.

When you emerge, everything is colorless. All the men wear long coats and crisp hats, and all the women wear dresses. You stop a woman on the street.

"Excuse me, miss, but I've traveled in a long tunnel without a lot of light. You look like you know where I can suss out some science."

You jerk your hand over your mouth. You have no idea why you spoke that way.

"Sure, but it'll cost you, see," the woman says. "Everything has a price."

You still can't believe what you're saying, but it starts to make sense. You've traveled to some black and white dimension, a parallel *noirniverse*. You search behind you for the portal but find nothing.

You die twelve years later while investigating the mysterious disappearance of Daisy Montgomery, heiress to the Montgomery Mill fortune.

The corrupt city mortician takes a long drag from his cigarette after uncovering your body.

"I've seen fewer holes in Swiss cheese. This is what it looks like when you get your beaker cleaned...by bullets."

THE END

You lurch toward the off-white and, miraculously, your body careens toward it. When you come to, dozens of well-dressed people crowd around you.

"Welcome to our planet, traveler. We are the people of Taupe."

The wormhole took you to an incredibly tasteful planet filled with refurbished vintage furniture and tasteful decor. The people there are always a little annoyed (and annoying), but they accept you as one of them because you were wearing your off-white lab coat (which has a few tasteful coffee stains).

As long as you search, you never find a portal back to your own world, so you start a new life on Taupe. You open a store called *Restoration Beaker* and sell artisanal beakers to people who want to put tasteful flowers in them. One day, a middle-aged woman taps you on the shoulder.

"I want to fill my beaker with some pebbles. Do you have a beaker sponge to clean with?"

You stare into the distance.

"I have no sponge. Mine is in another world. Another galaxy, perhaps. Another life."

The next day, you die. The mortician, as appointed by Taupe authorities, says your internal organs were almost identical to that of Taupians, though your brain was kind of small.

THE END

Dr. Masterson shows up, but you don't have time to think it through—you launch a poodle at him immediately. The poodle licks his lab coat and starts to bite, but then he drops to the floor.

"You fool," Masterson says. "What is a dog's one weakness?"

You realize your mistake.

"They can't read."

"No," he says and reaches into the dog's mouth. "They can't tolerate chocolate."

He pulls a half-eaten candy bar from the dog's mouth and eats it himself.

"I always carry it with me. Now what were you doing in here?"

"Little ol' me? Nothing at all."

But Masterson ignores your excuse, even though you suck on your thumb and try to look especially cute and vulnerable. He calls laboratory security (as well as a candy bar delivery service, which you didn't even realize was a thing).

You never do get Beatram back, and you never eat chocolate again either. Your life is filled with dreary days wishing you had come up with an incredibly clever excuse for being in the room. But alas, you did not.

The mortician says the bullet killed you instantly (in this life, you became a bodyguard for a powerful, yet surprisingly paternal, South American drug lord).

THE END

It's Dr. Masterson! You know that he'll punish you harshly unless you come up with the perfect excuse.

"I...like...beakers."

Masterson stares at you.

"How much?"

"So much. I like beakers. I like beakers!"

He bites his lip, but then he nods and smiles.

"I don't see any beakers or beaker-cleaning equipment in here, but I trust you. And I've come to draft you for a very special project."

"Good. Because I wasn't just in the air ducts, I swear."

He shuts the door and explains it all: he believes the lab has diverted money from their grants to fund a baking soda and vinegar operation, and he wants to blow the lid off the whole thing. You tune out during most of it, but for a second, you think he wants to fight you.

"These fists don't lie," you say and kiss your knuckles. "Put up your dukes."

"I said we have to fight for the truth, not fight each other."

"You're a sly one, Masterson, and I like that about you."

You give him a hug, and when he breaks away, he leads you out of the lab. He's got a plan, and you're going to give him a chance.

Turn to page 70.

You bring a poodle for Cacao to pet, and she does so unwillingly. You post the picture and watch the likes roll in.

"Three likes!" you say. "Not bad."

Cacao stares glumly and types.

"Not many likes. Cacao's piece about the evolution of NATO got mentioned in *New York Times*."

"OK, Cacao, I don't know who Nato is, but you have to forget about him and focus. We need more likes."

Cacao doesn't look happy. She types.

"Do not push Cacao. Cacao knows how to get more likes."

"Then do it, you idiotic ape!"

Cacao beats her mighty chest and you start to think you've made a mistake. Suddenly, she launches the poodle in the air, along with a banana. Then she picks you up by the heel and catapults you toward the ceiling.

You realize what's happening—Cacao is juggling. She keeps it up for a while, but she hasn't had much practice. You're the first item to be dropped, and since she threw you 30 feet in the air, you don't get up again.

The lab mortician has to scrape you off the floor. But he notes that Cacao's juggling pic did get 26 likes, which isn't bad.

THE END

You pull Cacao aside and smile.

"Cacao, I've got a real humdinger for you. That's human talk for a funny joke."

Cacao waits.

"Cacao, why do bananas wear suntan lotion? Because they peel! Type it in and watch the internet fame roll in, baby. Sorry, should I not have called you baby? I don't interact with many gorillae."

Cacao types.

"Your joke is a little hacky. Plus, the plural of gorilla is gorillas, not gorillae."

You grab Cacao by the fur.

"Just type the joke you dumb gorilla."

Cacao does as you say.

The first comment is a frowny face.

"Just give it a chance," you plead with the ape.

The second comment appears: *Lammmme*.

It turns out Cacao is more sensitive about her internet popularity than you realized. She kills you instantly, though the death is painless enough.

When the lab mortician comes in to clean up your body, he reads Cacao's screen. She's typed another joke.

What do you call a good scientist?

He gets to the punch line.

Dead.

Slowly, it registers.

"Cacao, that's a darn good joke!"

THE END

Cacao seems a little dumb, so you try to keep it simple.

"We need you to do something funny. Really funny."

Cacao nods like she understands, but instead of slipping on a banana peel or making a funny noise, she gets to work at her computer.

Weeks later, you return to find her large finger hovering over the *Upload* button. You stop her.

"Cacao, wait. What's your funny video? Did you go to the bathroom on something?"

Cacao types.

"Cacao reedited clips from *The Seventh Seal* to make it seem like romantic comedy. Juxtaposition of genres is humorous."

You try to break it to her gently.

"Cacao, that idea stinks. Do you need a banana peel or something?"

Cacao doesn't respond well to constructive criticism. She throws you out of the lab window and, too late, you realize that her room overhangs the lab's stock of poisonous hedges.

The lab mortician finds you days later, after the press tour for Cacao's viral video hit is over.

"Too bad," the mortician says. "The hedge wounds were bad, but not fatal. But then, for some reason, this scientist started eating hundreds of poisonous berries."

You'll never be hungry again.

THE END

You're nervous to ask Cacao to vlog, but she seems open to the idea—surprisingly open.

"Cacao loves self-expression," she types. "You offer true vehicle to expand Cacao's audience."

"Yeah sure, whatever."

"But Cacao needs you," she types. "Cacao needs your human voice."

You agree to team up with Cacao and help her vlog—she'll provide the script, editing, and acting, and you'll be the voice of the great ape.

You're immediately surprised by how prolific Cacao is. She churns out countless videos about accessible topics: *What Parents Don't Understand*; *My Parents Are So Weird*; and *Parents: Yuck Ugh Ew.* And you have to admit that you make a good team. Though Cacao occasionally gets upset when you ad-lib—she says your line, "Me gorilla, me stupid," doesn't fit with the rest of the video's tone— overall, it's a seamless partnership.

You become viral video hits, logging millions of views and making fives of dollars. Soon, the morning shows come calling. Fame is intoxicating, as is the free cough syrup they have in the green room.

After just a few months, a Las Vegas promoter calls. He wants you and Cacao to run a permanent show at the venue! You'll get to encourage destructive life choices like heavy drinking and gambling!

You spend years performing with Cacao, years you'll never get back. One day, your assistant knocks on the door.

"Former scientist, you have a visitor."

You snort some baking soda.

"If it's Bernie, tell him the buffet clause in my contract is non-negotiable."

Then you look up and begin to weep.

It's Beatram. He looks a little older and a little more worn, but it's him. And suddenly, you realize what you've become—a velour-wearing, baking soda-addicted monster.

Cacao knocks because it's show time, but when she sees you together with your beloved beaker sponge, she knows to leave. You turn to Beatram.

"I didn't know if you were alive. I had to move on."

Beatram is silent.

"Baby, I know I've changed. But we all put on weight. And the baking soda—I can quit. I can quit. I did it all for you!"

Beatram stares.

"But baby," you cry, "I was gonna come back. I was gonna come..."

You clutch your chest—the old ticker is finally going, and you've hurt the sponge you love the most.

The next morning, the casino mortician finds your body.

"Heart attack. Well, that's a lot less disgusting than the stuff I normally see around here!"

THE END

It may not be the smart thing. But you have a feeling it's the right thing. You raise the wall.

The vinegar rushes into the baking soda room and you finally realize how massive both reserves are. The fizz and foam breaks down the doors instantly, and you see everyone you know riding on the waves: the vaguely European scientist, some poodles, two good looking twins, an evil looking man with oddly compelling eyes, and many more. But someone else is missing.

The flood of baking soda and vinegar—also known as volcano juice—carries you to the highway.

"Algeria!" you shout. "Where are you, Algeria?"

You wander through the wreckage, searching for the revolutionary mouse. A few minutes later, you hear the sound of tiny feet in a puddle.

"Mon ami," he says, his voice barely a whisper. "I found the serum. But my vocal simulator is damaged. It may be—"

His voice cuts off. Now he's just like any other mouse with superintelligence and a beret. But he's pulling something behind him, and he hands it to you.

"Beatram!" you cry. "You found Beatram!"

Algeria squeaks once more.

"Viva the revolution!" you shout.

The tiny mouse scurries into the foam and you hold your beloved sponge, wet with volcano juice, close to your shaking chest.

THE END

You decide not to trust the genius talking mouse, despite his beret. You hit the alarm and Algeria closes his eyes.

"I would kill you," he says, his accent stronger than ever. "But you deserve to suffer living with what you've done."

The mouse flees and you're left alone with the shrieking alarm. Security finds and arrests you and, surprisingly, they don't believe you when you tell them that it was the talking mouse's fault.

You're banned from the laboratory for life, and you find it hard to scrape by in a world where people want employees to be competent. For a while, you hold down a job as a dog washer, but after you call too many dogs "Beaker," they let you go.

You never do reunite with Beatram, the beaker sponge you once called your friend. You die twelve years later, when the Fake Science Labs accidentally puts baking soda and vinegar in your water pipes and your entire apartment explodes.

The mortician visits your home, but he can't find your body amidst the volcano juice.

"It's sad," he tells his wife later that night. "They said that scientist was one of the best beaker cleaners in the world. Now, there's just a spot on the rug."

THE END

"No!" you scream as you throw up your hands. "Explosive poison is terrible for my complexion!"

You block the poison—but too late, you realize how you did it.

Beatram shakes. He's absorbed all of the explosive poison. You squeeze him.

"You can make it. You can make it buddy!"

Beatram explodes.

You collapse to the floor, your face covered in sponge viscera.

"Give me the rest," you cry to Cothree.

"Don't you want to stop my horrific plan?"

"What's the point of living?"

Cothree gives you the rest of the poison and you swallow it all. At first, it's hard to tell if you'll explode or be poisoned, but you faint before you can find out.

Cothree calls the lab mortician immediately after you die.

"I tried to help this poor scientist," the evil Cothree says, "but I was too late."

"Wow," the mortician says. "The poison was definitely explosive. But why are there pieces of sponge in the guts pile?"

Cothree shrugs.

"Maybe from eating a sponge? I don't know, that scientist was pretty dumb."

"Case closed!" the mortician shouts, and he and Cothree high-five.

THE END

124

"Not this time, you oddly compelling jerk!"

You launch yourself at Cothree, Beatram leading the charge as you thrust your right hand forward. Cothree's caught off-guard and ends up with a mouthful of sponge. You take what remains of the explosive poison and pour it on Cothree. His compelling eyes shut.

"We're not done, Beatram." You embrace your faithful sponge. "We're going to make things right."

You can't leave the lab without destroying the system that Cothree has put in place. No lab should profit from volcanoes—that's part of the scientist's code that you just made up.

You run into the hallway and look around—there has to be some science somewhere, but you don't see any options. You start opening doors at random, but all your find are some poodles, a movie set, an uninviting inter-dimensional portal, and some overly enthusiastic twins.

This is bigger than you or Beatram. You turn to your faithful sponge.

"The question is, what do we do now, old chum?"

Beatram suggests something you never even considered.

"I guess we could clean beakers," you reply. "But what about stopping the lab's plan?"

Beatram considers it, and he has a point.

"True," you say. "We are best at cleaning beakers. But how can we use that skill to save the lab, nay, the world?"

Beatram doesn't understand.

"No, not neigh like a horse," you tell him. "Nay like *no*. I learned it from that guy we just killed. But what do you think we should do? I think we need to fight."

Beatram still doesn't agree.

"But Beatram," you protest, "I protest. How will cleaning beakers help us? We need to get out the big guns and fight."

Beatram hardens in response.

"Yes," you say, "of course I trust you. But I just don't understand your plan."

You return to the room where you first began this long journey, and an alarm goes off instantly. Beatram still wants to clean.

It's taking too long, and you know from experience that you and your beloved beaker sponge could end up arguing all night. It's time to make a decision.

Will you try to fight the lab and take it down through sheer force? Or will you take Beatram's advice and go back to cleaning beakers?

To take out the lab through any means necessary, turn to page 136.

To clean beakers with Beatram, turn to page 146.

You decide, like all great heroes, to make a run for it.

You spend the first 20 feet trying to remember if the T-rex can see you when you move or stand still, but since you can't remember, you try both.

After quickly moving and not-moving for a few feet, you get into a serious rhythm. You begin to dance away from the growling beast.

As you feel its warm breath on your neck, you can't help but think you should start a career as a professional background dancer. You have the goods to make it work, and you can do it under pressure! With these rhythms and your ability to learn choreography while maintaining your own sense of self-expression, you'd make an exciting part of any traveling dance group.

The T-rex eats you.

The lab mortician is eaten by the T-rex as well, so he never does find your body. However, when the *Guinness Book of Records* reviews the videotape of your death a few years later, they name you the first person to be eaten while doing the Electric Slide.

THE END

Taming a Tyrannosaurus rex seems absurd, but you don't have much other choice. You have to approach it carefully—the beast has never been tamed by a human, so only the most precise and careful technique will allow you to survive.

You hop onto its back and shout "Giddy-up!" into its ear holes.

At first, the great animal tries to buck you off, at least when it isn't eating other random humans. But that gives you time to fashion an elaborate system of ferns that you weave into reins, a saddle, and a very nice pair of pants.

Slowly, the T-rex bends to your will, feeling the pull of your fern reins upon his great neck. It turns out that it's kind of easy to train such a stupid animal. After a few minutes, you name him.

"Fido, if you dare buck me again, I shall inflict great pain upon you."

He whimpers.

"Good, Fido. Always obey me, your incredibly intelligent and inedible master."

He nods his mighty head, sending your entire body up and down with it. Now you have to guide Fido somewhere else. At first, he tramples over a few more small buildings and indistinct humans, but then you reach a clearing in the Cretaceous Amusement Area where it's possible to see the whole lab and the vast industrial wasteland that lies just beyond the suburbs.

Turn to the next page.

"One day, Fido, all of this shall be yours."

Fido roars, but you hit your forehead.

"I just realized I gave you a name people use for dogs. What do you think about Rover instead?"

He shakes his head and roars again.

"Fido it is. But now we have to figure out what to do."

Fido is a faithful companion, except for his refusal to stop eating humans.

"It's like the old saying," you note. "Well, I'm sure there's an old saying somewhere. Anyway, we have more important things to do than going through a quote book."

Fido makes a whimper that you can only interpret as, "Tell me more, intelligent and physically-attractive master."

Fido lets you off his back during his periodic human-eating breaks.

"You're one of the best dinosaurs I've ever tamed and ridden, old chum, but I have a friend who is even closer to me than you. His name is Beatram, he's a beaker sponge, and we have to save him."

Fido rushes toward the large network of buildings, but you pull hard on his ferny reins.

"Whoa boy. I'm not sure of the right approach. Do you think we should destroy the lab and find Beatram that way? Or should we scare everyone out and ask them to give us back our beloved sponge?"

Fido still proves to be rather dumb, since all he does is roar. This is a decision you'll have to make yourself.

To stomp the lab with extreme force, turn to page 137.

To threaten the employees, turn to page 139.

You pet the cat nearest to you and smile cruelly.

"Get in the box, you fools." Your voice is gravelly and an octave deeper (because you have a severe cat allergy). "Get in the bloody box."

Devin sighs as you furiously rub your eyes.

"Are you an *Oliver Twist* character now?"

"Guv'nah, do as I bloody say!"

Emma climbs in the box.

"What are you going to do to us?"

"I'm goin' ta' bloody off you blokes!"

"OK," Devin says, "anything to stop that accent. But would you do us a favor first?"

You consider it—it doesn't seem like a good idea to do a favor for the people you're about to kill, but you want them to still like you.

"I'll grant you one bloody favor, you Guv'nahs. I like figgy pudding.'"

Devin hands you a beaker.

"My sister and I are really into soda, so we made this. It has lots of sugar in it and tastes like candy. And guess what? We're serving it in a beaker."

You stop rubbing your eyes and open them. It's hard to see anything at the moment, but you're no fool: sugar is hard to pass up, and candy is even better. The fact that it's in a beaker sweetens the deal—maybe literally.

"Is the beaker made of sugar, Guv'nah?"

"What? Why?"

"I need to check if it sweetens the deal...literally."

"Oh just kill us," Emma says. "Let's not even bother."

"Yes!" Devin shouts over her. "It's made of sugar."

You cackle, mad with power, your eyes, mouth and nostrils filled with powerful cat hair.

"Give me the bloody beaker!"

Devin hands the beaker to you, and though you can't see its label or contents, you happily slurp. But something's wrong—the sugar flavoring is too subtle. You collapse on a pile of cats.

"You bloody Guv'nahs, what have you done to me?"

Through a blur, you can see Devin and Emma leave the box.

"Thanks for being part of our experiment," they say at the same time. "And thanks for drinking explosive poison."

You gasp—you can feel it taking hold.

"Twins...are...so...creepy," you scream as you explode.

The lab mortician is called in to clean up your body.

"My wife and I are having a party Sunday night. You want to come?" he asks Devin as he sweeps up the cat hair.

"Thanks for the invite. She models, right?"

"Oh yeah," the mortician says as he discards your entrails. "Just got a catalog thing. Still mostly sweaters."

THE END

"I am not a vengeful ruler," you proclaim. "I am just."

You start sneezing a lot because of your severe cat allergy, but you have greater concerns. There's no need to get revenge on Devin and Emma—you have an entire laboratory to save.

"Felines, assemble!"

The cats line up in front of you, ready to do your bidding, since cats are famous for their willingness to take orders from humans.

"Now we deal with Emma and Devin."

The twins bow before you, but you wave them away (while sneezing, so a bit of mucus flies in their direction).

"I seek not your punishment, but your redemption. Did I say that right?"

The twins nod.

"Anyway," you continue, "I want to find my beaker sponge. Beatram is somewhere in this laboratory, and you're going to tell me how to find him."

"And if we don't?" Devin asks.

"Do the right thing for once. For me. For science."

Devin turns to his sister and she nods. He begins to explain it all.

"If you hit the lab's supply of baking soda and vinegar, you'll stop everything. It's where all the cash comes from, and they'll have to give you your sponge back. Without the ability to make volcano juice, the lab is completely crippled."

"Of course," you say. "It makes perfect sense, if

you don't think about it too hard."

"The question is simple," Emma says as you rub your eyes and sneeze. "How do you take the lab out?"

"You have two options," Devin says. "You can do it yourself, or you can send the cats to do it for you."

"What do you mean?"

"Simple. You go to the vinegar room and figure out how to dump the vat onto the baking soda. Or, we train the cats to go through the air ducts and do it for us."

"And why are you so willing to help?"

"You could have killed us," Devin says. "And you're so allergic that the cats will probably kill you anyway."

Emma smiles at you.

"We're all scientists here."

You cough a little.

"No, Emma. I am but a beaker cleaner searching for his sponge."

Devin nods.

"Then let's find it."

To trust your excellent counting skills and do it yourself, turn to page 140.

To train the cats, turn to page 141.

You bravely broadcast everything about the lab: the conspiracies, the secrets, and the ambiguity about the 401(k) plan. But nobody sees it because the final episode of *America's Next Top Body Part* is on that night (the buttocks get second place).

In case you were curious, America's Next Top Body Part is...the elbow!!!

You're banned from the lab and never again see the sponge that used to know all of your top body parts. You gaze at beakers in shop windows and tell children to never fall in love.

Four years later, you are the first contestant to die on *America's Top Weird People Desperate For Money*. When she sees your body, the show's mortician says, "They aren't paying me enough for this."

THE END

"Sorry, Doc," you tell old Masterson. "I've made the mistake of leaving my sponge before. I won't do it again. You're on your own."

The security camera doesn't say the number of the room, but that's a good thing, since you might be confused by anything larger than eight. Anyway, you'd recognize the place anywhere—it's the same room where you cleaned beakers when this crazy day began.

You rush through the hallways, stopping only to avoid other scientists, check your email, watch a short television program called *America's Next Top Body Part*, and take a nap. You can't slow down, so after another side trip to the lab cafeteria, a pit stop at the gift shop, and a brief chat with the financial advisor about the status of your 401(k) should you betray and/or explode the lab, you make it to the room full of beakers.

Beatram's right there on the counter, just as you'd seen on camera. You pick him up and an alarm goes off almost instantly.

"Beatram, no! Did you betray me?"

Beatram explains that the lab knew you were on the loose and wanted to lure you in. The question is what to do next. You want to flee—but Beatram has a stranger suggestion. He wants you to clean beakers.

To escape the lab completely, turn to page 144.

To clean beakers with Beatram, turn to page 146.

"We shall fight!" you shout at Beatram. "I'm not going with your wimpy plan. I'm going to fix this lab forever. For science!"

The only problem is that you aren't really sure where to start. You've never destroyed an entire lab before, so you search the room for a manual. You only find books about tax evasion, litigation strategy, and routes to international waters.

You're running out of time, so you flee the room and wander the hallways, sponge in hand. But then you see them.

A gaggle of guard poodles are barking and they've never looked more well-groomed and upset. You throw up a hand.

"Stop, guard poodles. Listen to my case. I believe we can stop what the lab is doing and help all mankind."

The poodles don't listen. Beatram tries to stop them from gnawing upon your tender limbs, but he can only do so much.

The lab mortician finds your remains a few minutes later, and even he's surprised to find that such well-groomed dogs could be so vicious.

THE END

"Stomp it!" you command Fido. "Stomp it all!"

He demonstrates a surprisingly adept understanding of the English language and begins to stomp. Using his massive weight and impressive feet, he kicks at the buildings with glee.

You watch as the concrete walls crumble under Fido's force. You whisper to the great beast.

"They look like ants from up here, Fido. Tiny scientists, running from us. But nothing can save them now."

Fido stomps on the occasional tiny scientist, as well as a few even tinier scientists, but you don't mind. A few people have to suffer for the sake of progress, especially when it's a large, recently-trained T-rex making that progress.

You see figures familiar from your time in the lab—the napkin bandana guy, the mean scientist, and the other mean scientist. But at one point, Fido hesitates. You jerk back the ferns.

"Onward you brute! We have to stomp it all."

He stomps one building and you watch as a strange white powder collects on his taloned foot. It looks like the entire room was filled with powder.

"Don't slow down," you scream into Fido's ear holes. "Not now. We're just beginning. Stomp on that vinegar-smelling room next to it, and stomp vigorously."

Fido hesitates, so you pull the ferns hard. He stomps.

Turn to the next page.

A flood of vinegar pours onto the white powder. You realize what you've done.

"Oh no. Fido, you fool! I can smell that sweet white powder from here. It's baking soda! You've made volcano juice!"

The foamy explosion knocks both of you backward and you fall onto the grass. You make sure none of the volcano juice gets on your lab coat, but that is a mistake—it makes you particularly appetizing to Fido.

He looks at you with sad eyes. Then he eats you whole. Unfortunately, you only survive a few days in his stomach before dying.

The lab mortician never finds your body because he dies in the flood of volcano juice.

Beatram never learns what happened to his friend, and he thinks you abandoned him—which, in a way, is true. Your anger made you leave your closest friend behind.

Fido retires to the Berkshires.

THE END

You command Fido to run to the entrance of the lab.

From atop your reptilian steed, you can see the full majesty of the industrial wasteland and bombed out suburb where this lab, like all Fake Science Labs, is located. Just beyond the horizon, the roof of a forgotten mall glints in the smoggy daylight.

"Once," you whisper to Fido, "that held a Spencer's Gifts."

The two of you reach the front of the laboratory. You tug on the ferns and Fido knows exactly what to do. He lets loose a mighty roar and the doors open. Scientists pour out, large and tiny alike. You immediately recognize the vaguely European scientist who promoted you in the first place.

"What do you want?" she asks, still rather imposing. "Whatever it is, we'll give it to you. Just put the dinosaur down. You know what? We'll give you our full patent portfolio. What do you think of that? The whole lab is yours. Just please, let us be."

You'd never considered the full patent portfolio, since you don't know what it it, but it sounds appealing and expensive. Yet part of you thinks you should go back to what you know best: cleaning beakers with your sponge.

To obtain the lab's patent portfolio, turn to page 145.

To clean beakers with Beatram, turn to page 146.

You've made mistakes in the past, but you've proven yourself by now. It's time to go on the hunt by yourself.

Within five minutes, you're completely lost. You try retracing your steps, but the floor is too clean to see them. You're lost.

You do manage to find the cafeteria, so you order a quick Salisbury steak, a side of potatoes, some brownies, and a soda.

By the time you finish, you've lost track of your assignment. Where were you going again? Were you planning on doing something about your 401(k)? Or were you going to see if any tiny scientists wanted to hang out or be stepped on?

A food coma overcomes you, but it quickly turns out to be a literal coma, thanks to the dangerous combination of radioactive isotopes in the brownies. The cafeteria's head chef should be fired, but if you could speak, even you would admit that it was a tasty recipe.

Unfortunately, you don't make it. The lab mortician dissects you in front of a small group of interns.

"So here's the appendix," he says, holding yours up. "Just trash this."

You did not die with dignity.

THE END

"Cats ho!" you shout before sneezing, and the felines vault into the air ducts. You hear their tiny paws scampering above.

You shout into your walkie-talkie.

"Cats, are you infiltrating the room?"

From across the room, you hear a response.

"Devin, go get the other walkie-talkie, I heard something."

Devin grabs the walkie-talkie and hands it to you.

"Cats, can you hear me?" you say into the device.

"Cats can you hear me?" the other device plays back.

"Darn it," you say and shake your head. "I don't understand what message they're trying to get through. They're repeating me."

Emma sighs.

"Do you really think cats can talk?"

"Didn't you hear them?"

"Did you even give one of the cats a walkie-talkie?"

"Of course not. I wanted both in case the first one failed."

She takes the walkie-talkies from you.

"We have no choice but to wait."

You can't believe it.

"Does this mean we can play hacky sack?"

The three of you relive the old times playing hacky sack, though Devin isn't as good as he used to be. It turns out that losing an arm can do weird

Turn to the next page.

*Mars Ball! What a game! Anyway, you're dead,
but watch Xlanor Tribiday perfectly hit the Mars
Ball with her Mars Bat!*

things to your balance. Still, you shout at him to step up his game.

But you don't have time to play much longer. You hear a rush of noise coming from the hallways, followed by a crashing sound.

"They did it!" Emma shouts. "The baking soda and vinegar!"

"Volcano juice!" you scream as the door falls.

You watch as the volcano juice rushes in, cats riding atop the waves. The next thing you know, you've been pushed far from the lab and are in an empty field.

"What happened?" you mutter. "Where am I? And why do I feel compelled to narrate my thoughts?"

You can barely move your head, but you turn left. And then you see it. Half of the sponge you call Beatram.

He's broken, but he's alive. You nurse him to health as best you can, but some things cannot be undone. As the years go by, you can't clean beakers together—Beatram isn't strong enough. But you clean many test tubes, and you clean them well.

You die 68 years later, in a small colony on Mars. Your last words are to Beatram.

"It only took half of you to make me whole."

The colony mortician says, "Wow, that was a pretty old person. Well, back to playing Mars Ball (it's a popular game on Mars)!"

THE END

"Forget that, Beats! We're getting out of here."

You are too scared to clean beakers, and if you've learned anything, it's that courage is severely overrated.

You flee the room, Beatram in hand, and scan the hallway for a way out. You run as quickly as you can, occasionally hitting a few walls (you've never been obsessed with coordination).

Unfortunately, you don't make it far. It turns out you've been running in a giant circle, giving lab security more than enough time to find you and track you down. The security guards cuff you and strip Beatram away. The guard shouts at you.

"This is, in a way, a fitting punishment for what I assume was cowardice."

"Yep," the other guard shouts, staring at Beatram, "I can only assume it's a fitting reflection, in some small way, of a cosmic karmic code."

"Say that three times fast!" the guard shouts and laughs. They throw you out of the laboratory.

You go on to have a successful career as a bartender at a bar that serves all the drinks in test tubes. But you never do see Beatram again, and you always think of him when you serve the signature drink that bears his name (baking soda, water, and pieces of sponge).

You die 12 years later in a bar fight. The bar wins. The city mortician says you were a fool to think you could beat an inanimate object.

THE END

You consider it carefully. It seems like a mistake to abandon the most important thing in your life, but on the other hand, money.

"I'll take it!" you shout.

You take the lab's patent portfolio and are immediately contacted by 400 different law firms. It turns out that you're suddenly wanted for child endangerment, abuse of the patent system, systemic asbestos hoarding, insider trading of volcano stocks, and, worst of all, beaker endangerment.

"I give it all back!" you tell the vaguely European scientist. "I just wanted to make money without effort or consequence!"

"Not so fast," she says. "You signed a contract."

She shows you a 300 page document with your signature on each page. You recognize it.

"I thought that was just a formality."

"That's what contracts are. Formalities."

You're sent to jail for failure to understand the charges brought against you. Though you find some solace cleaning license plates with a dirty rag, it's not like it was with Beatram.

You die seven months later by drowning (the prison has a really deep pool and, for the record, a great pool program, but you lied and told them you could swim).

The prison mortician says you have nice hands, so he takes them home with him.

THE END

146

The outside world is nothing to you now. You hear nothing, and your ears fill with silence like you're underwater. There's a reason why: you're here to clean beakers.

"Beatram," you say to your trusty sponge, "let's get to work."

Like a bow across the strings of a violin, you wipe Beatram across the lip of the beaker.

"Kiss the lip," you say, "kiss it my sweet sponge."

You watch as the residue disappears and the beaker is clean. Part of you hears an alarm going off, but you ignore it to continue cleaning. But you need one thing.

Before you were whisked away in the beginning of this long journey, they refused to give you baking soda. This time, you don't ask. You search the cabinets and, with Beatram's help, you find a full box. You give it a smell.

"It still gets me high," you tell the sponge. "High on cleaning."

You douse Beatram with water and dust on your cleaning agent of choice. You wipe some tiny scientists from the beaker and try to let it all sink in, whatever may come. As you clean the second beaker, the doors burst open. You continue cleaning.

You can tell that armed guards have charged in, but you ignore them. You hear the vaguely European scientist, but you ignore her as well. Around you, you can feel that hundreds of people have rushed into the laboratory, but instead of shouting and stopping your efforts, they stand in stunned silence.

Finally, the vaguely European scientist speaks, and she has tears in her eyes.

"This is what you are doing?" she asks you.

You lift Beatram from his beaker lip kiss.

"This is not what I do," you say, your voice but a whisper. "This is who I am."

She begins to weep, and the other scientists do the same. You see everyone from your time in the laboratory, but you only know the beakers.

You clean and the group watches in rapture as you go from one beaker to the next, you and Beatram in perfect harmony together. His pores mold to your fingers and your movements pace to his spongy rhythm. The moment breaks when the vaguely European scientist speaks.

"I hereby declare an emergency meeting of the board."

A few scientists shuffle forward, their eyes as teary as everyone else's. The scientist speaks, her vaguely European accent stronger than ever before.

"Today, I have seen the excellence that I sought when I came to this laboratory. And I have seen it in a lowly beaker cleaner. So I propose that we make a change in honor of that."

"Go on!" the crowd shouts. You're a little bored, so you sniff some baking soda, but then you continue to listen.

"My passion is the search for truth. The quest for higher things. And this beaker cleaner has done that

Turn to the next page.

with a simple beaker sponge and baking soda. So I ask that we immediately reallocate our entire baking soda supply to this incredible team."

One scientist in the back shouts.

"But what about the volcano juice?"

"We will do something else." She turns to you. "Will you lead us now?"

You have tears in your eyes, but you can speak.

"I...like...beakers."

The laboratory bursts into applause.

You become the first chair of the lab's Beaker Cleaning Institute, and Beatram becomes vice-chair. Students from around the world come to learn from how you clean. Tuition is more than enough to make up for the lost volcano juice money, and you and Beatram become living legends. The lab even upgrades your 401(k) to a 501(k).

Though your life could have taken many paths, you have a sense that this is the one true ending, and that everything else is sort of a sham in comparison. You have won at life.

40 years later, you and Beatram die on the same day, cleaning beakers. The lab dedicates a statue in your honor, and your institute lives on for millennia.

The lab mortician speaks at your funeral.

"Let us dwell not on death. But let us dwell on the beaker cleaner's creed."

Thousands chant the same phrase.

"I...like...beakers!

THE END

HERE LIES A BEAKER CLEANER AND A SPONGE.
TO BE CLEAR, EVEN THOUGH THIS IS A GRAVESTONE, THEY HAD A HAPPY AND FULFILLING LIFE TOGETHER, SO THIS IS ALL MUCH MORE TRIUMPHANT THAN IT SEEMS.

YOU CAN HELP SCIENCE!

Did this book change your life completely?
Of course!

So help us bring you more stories in the
legendary *Make Your Own Mistakes* series.

When you write a review of the book where you
bought it, you make it easier for us to produce
another. It takes a second, costs nothing, and
helps more people make mistakes!

Thank you for supporting our efforts instead of
some charity!

ABOUT THE AUTHOR

Phil Edwards is the author of the *Make Your Own Mistakes* series and the textbook *Fake Science 101*. An accomplished transcriptionist at the Fake Science Laboratories, he has advanced degrees in typing. A true adventurer, he travels between the lab's many locations, from the suburbs of Detroit, to the suburbs of Cleveland, and even to the suburbs of Phoenix.

You can learn more about the laboratory at FakeScience.org.

Please note, we did not have a photography budget for this book, so we could not take a picture of Edwards. However, we did have an extra avocado drawing. Feel free to imagine that it not only tastes delicious, but also wrote this book.

43646220R00091

Made in the USA
San Bernardino, CA
21 December 2016